BUSINESS ENGLISH

AN INDIVIDUALISED LEARNING PROGRAMME

PETER WILBERG   MICHAEL LEWIS

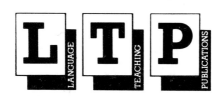

Language Teaching Publications
35 Church Road Hove BN 3 2BE

ISBN   Bound edition   0 906717 72 8
          Looseleaf edition   0 906717 79 5

Printed in England by Commercial Colour Press, London E7.

Business English is based on an idea by Peter Wilberg. The materials have been developed
by Peter Wilberg and Michael Lewis. The cross-cultural material was contributed by Philip
O'Connor of Language Training Services in consultation with Michael Lewis.

Acknowledgements

We are grateful for permission to reproduce the newspaper articles on pages 48 and 92.
The front cover was designed by Deb Durban, based on a picture from the Zefa Picture
Library (UK).

Copyright

CONTENTS

HOW TO GET THE BEST OUT OF YOUR COURSE AND THIS BOOK

On these two pages are some general guidance to help you learn efficiently and effectively.

1. Set yourself objectives before you begin your course. Decide what you need to learn. Make a plan. How much time can you give each day/week to improving your English?

2. **Either** follow the plan **or** change it, but **don't** forget it. Approach improving your English in the same way you approach a carefully designed project at work:

set objectives   make a timetable   review progress   revise objectives

3. Remember, a lot of your work will be wasted if you do not keep a good record of what you learn. Record the new language you need **accurately** and in a way that you can **recover** the information. The carefully designed pages of this book will help you to organise what you learn so that you can find the language you need later.

4. Remember, it is a waste of time to record information unless you can find it again when you need it. A list of **all** the new words from your English class is often almost useless, because you will not be able to find the word you need a few weeks later!

5. It is difficult to remember things arranged in lists (try to learn a few lines of the telephone book!). It is better to arrange the new words and phrases you learn in other ways, which make them easier to remember. This book suggests some effective ways of arranging new language.

6. It is easier to remember new language if you write a sentence which uses the new word. It is even better if the sentence is your own personal sentence. Choose one which is true, about yourself or a friend, or perhaps an amusing sentence. All these ways will help you to remember the new words better.

7. After you have written your sentences, say them aloud. Say them more than once, until they seem natural to you. It is important that you feel happy when you say the new sentences. That helps you to remember better, too.

8. When you feel natural with a new sentence, say it once again. This time record it, in your own voice, on a cassette tape. Later, when you are doing nothing — perhaps when you are driving your car — listen to the tape. Many people learn very efficiently by listening to their own voices!

9. When you are working with your teacher, don't worry about making mistakes. When you make a mistake it helps the teacher to help you. It is very difficult to help students who worry too much about making mistakes.

10. Not all mistakes are very important. Mistakes are important if somebody mis-understands what you mean, or if somebody thinks you are rude or aggressive when you do not mean to be. Some mistakes are important to **you** because they make you feel silly. If you think a mistake is important make a careful note of it (see pages 120 to 126) and then make a special effort to avoid those mistakes later.

11. One of the best ways to improve is for you to **try to say** what you want, and then for your teacher to tell you the **best** way of saying that naturally. When your teacher helps you like this, write down the **exact** words, then look back regularly until you are confident that you can use the natural language yourself.

12. This book should be a record of **all the important language you learn** on your course. That should make it very valuable. Take care of it and use it regularly!

CLASSROOM ENGLISH

Many people who are studying business English are studying it with a teacher, either alone or in a small group. These classes provide a real opportunity to practise English which is important in real business situations. You can use the classroom like a business meeting — not like a classroom. Forget that there is a 'teacher' and 'students'; instead, think of all the people as participants in a business meeting. Both the teacher and the student(s) should use the language in class which is normally used in business. Treat the class as a meeting and practise interrupting, changing the subject, asking for more details etc. using businesslike language. Here are some useful expressions:

Shall we begin by looking at....
I wonder if it might be helpful/a good idea to....

Would you like me to go over that again/in more detail?
Could you go over that again/in more detail, please?

Are you sure?
Really?
Could you be more specific?

I'm not sure I completely understand/agree.
I wonder if that's the best way/if there's a better way of doing that.

Excuse me, could I just ask a question/make a point before you/we go on?
I think we'd better leave that until a later/our next meeting.
I'm not sure this is the right time to discuss that question.

I'll let you have a summary of what we have said today/tomorrow/in a few days.
Do you think you could just let me have a few notes about what we've said today please.

N otice all this language is like the language of a business meeting, not the language of a language lesson! Use your lessons to practise for meetings.

LEARNING ENGLISH

Nobody is quite sure how we learn. Some people seem to learn best in one way and other people in a different way. But there are some general principles which will help you. Often in this book you will find expert help. There are short notes which will make your studying more effective. They look like this:

Don't just list every new word you meet. Choose words you think are important for you.

Don't just list one form of a word; make sure you know the family of words:

produce (verb)	product (noun)	production (noun)
productivity (noun)	producer (noun)	

Try to make an example sentence about your job or your own life for each of the words in the word family. This will help you to remember them better.

IDENTIFYING YOUR NEEDS

There are two important steps to improving your English for professional reasons.

1. Identifying the language you need.

2. Recording what you learn in the most effective way.

Before you begin, you need to think about these things carefully. In business you plan before you do anything. You want to avoid wasting time, money and work. It is the same with your foreign language study. You need to plan, to set yourself clear objectives, and to work in an organised, efficient and effective way. Planning is not wasting time. It is an important part of your study programme.

This book helps you to discover your language needs and objectives. After you have done that, it helps if you study effectively and record what you learn in the most useful way. This first section of the book is very important. It is designed to help you to plan your learning programme. Use it carefully. Don't rush. It will help you to discover the things which it is most important and helpful for you to learn. Take your time. You are making an important investment!

Fill in the tables on the next few pages. If you can, do this in English. You can also complete them in your own language. It is more important to complete these pages fully and accurately, than to do it in English. These pages are not to test your English. They are to help you, and your teacher, to discover the English you need.

1

NEEDS 1 — TOPICS

Complete the table below as fully as possible. Use your own language or English or both.
Use the ideas at the top of the page to help you, but think carefully of **why** you need English
and **how** you need to use English. Think of your job and of yourself, and your personal
needs and interests.

I NEED ENGLISH FOR:

banking   *sales*   *finance*   *meeting
                                                            visitors*

　　import/export   *accountancy*   *advertising*
?   *?*   *agriculture*
　personnel management   *economics*   *retail trade*
                                                            ?
　　　　travel   *?*   *computers*
                                                            entertaining

NEED	DETAILS
1	
2	
3	
4	
5	

NEEDS 2 — FUNCTIONS

Which of these things do you need to do in English? Give as many details as possible. Remember, you can use English or your own language.

I NEED TO DO THESE THINGS IN ENGLISH:

greet visitors
suggestion
make a complaint
make small talk
discuss proposals
contracts
problems

? express my opinion
request
agree and disagree

present my company
graphs
our product
talk about figures
our plans
money

describe people
plans
?
jobs
products
places
talk on the phone
interrupt

answer questions
compare things

NEED	DETAILS
Things I do often in English	
1	
2	
3	
I don't do it often, but it is very important.	
Something special I am going to do soon in English.	

1

NEEDS 3 — SITUATIONS

If you want to discover the language you need it will help if you think about the different situations when you use English. The language you need changes from place to place and from person to person. Use the suggested words to help to describe as carefully as possible when and where you use English.

WHO DO YOU SPEAK ENGLISH TO?	clients	customers
	colleagues	technicians
	responsibility	superiors
	secretarial staff	bosses
	nationality	????

WHAT ABOUT?	products	arrangements
	plans	deals
	prices	discounts
	promotions	supplies

WHY?	reporting	buying
	agreeing	selling
	discussing	reviewing
	presenting	introducing

WHERE AND WHEN?	country	place
	factory	office
	conference	trade fair
	meeting	social contacts

HOW DO YOU USE ENGLISH?	telephone	face-to-face
	one-to-one	groups
	meetings	in writing
	telex	????

HOW DO YOU MEET ENGLISH REGULARLY?	private reading
	company literature
	TV radio
	professional press
	contact with native English/American speakers

NEEDS 4 — DAILY ROUTINE

Think about how you spend a typical day. Fill in things which you do regularly. Use English as much as possible; use your own language if necessary. This diary page might help you to think of more occasions when you use English for your job. Use the suggestions to help you. Underline all the things you do in English.

A TYPICAL DAY

	Morning	Lunch time	Afternoon	Evening

YESTERDAY

	Morning	Lunch time	Afternoon	Evening

analysing	meeting	planning	explaining	listening to .....
phoning	arranging	liaising with	checking	visiting .....
socialising with	instructing	thinking about	interviewing	relaxing .....
reviewing	consulting	writing	negotiating	travelling .....

Which five activities on this list do you do most often in English?

NEEDS 5 — ANNUAL ROUTINE

Probably your job changes at different times of year. But most of us operate an annual cycle; things happen regularly at the same time of year. Use the year planner below to list regular events in your calendar. Underline the ones when you use English. Does it help you to discover more of your language needs?

JANUARY

FEBRUARY

MARCH

APRIL

MAY

JUNE

NEEDS 6 — ANNUAL ROUTINE

JULY

AUGUST

SEPTEMBER

OCTOBER

NOVEMBER

DECEMBER

Think of all the national holidays that you have in your own country. Fill them in on the calendar in English. Here are some of the expressions you may need

New Years Day	**Easter**	**Christmas**
Annual Holidays	**May Day**	**Religious Holiday**

The more detail you put on your calendar, the more it will help you to think of situations when you use your English. The calendar can help you and your teacher to identify more of your language needs.

1

YOUR LANGUAGE NEEDS

A large part of this book will help you to identify and list **word partnerships** which are particularly useful for you. This page explains how and why learning word partnerships will help you.

Here is a simple, general example. If you think of football the first word which comes to mind is probably **ball**. If you think of more 'football words' you will probably choose **nouns** like **match, team**. Most people choose nouns. Often we start to think about a topic by starting with important nouns.

In business English you probably think first of words like **advert** or **sales.** But when we want to talk about something we need to know the **verbs** which often make a **word partnership** with the noun.

You can't talk about a game of football unless you know the words which are often used with **ball:**

head a ball	**kick the ball**	**pass the ball**
lob the ball	**throw the ball**	

From **one** useful noun, we can identify **a group** of useful verbs.

Another kind of word partnership in English is made by making a partnership of two nouns:

football match	**football supporter**	**football ground**
football season	**football league**	**football club**

You can see that from one word we can cover a very wide area by identifying **word partnerships**.

It is the same with the business words:

place an advert;	**appoint an advertising agency;**	
increase sales;	**a sales conference;**	**launch a sales campaign**.

Pages 57 to 76 will help you to create **your own personalised word partnership** lists.

From a few words, your teacher can help you to identify a lot of language you will find immediately useful to talk about your professional and personal interests.

Time spent identifying the language which is most useful for you is not wasted. The process of thinking about, and talking about your needs will help you to learn English efficiently.

INTRODUCTION

2

Every professional needs to talk about their work. But we are not usually happy talking to people if we know nothing about them. In different countries people talk more or less about themselves, their families and their interests when they are meeting people professionally. But everyone needs to be able to say something about themselves. The next few pages will help you to say something about yourself in English. You can complete the pages you think will be useful for you. If you are not happy to answer the questions – don't answer them. You do not need to say anything you are not happy to say.

These pages are to help you to say what you want to say. Please use them in that way.

On page 150 you will find ideas to help you think about the topics which you think professional people can talk about with contacts that they do not know very well. Remember, these are often different in different parts of the world, but finally, what you want to talk about is for you to decide!

In addition to talking about your professional life, you can help a teacher to help you find the personal language you need by using some of these things:

A CV /Resumé

Photographs

A map/guide of your home town/region

YOURSELF

2

Complete the following sentences about yourself.

I was born in	_____ (place)
in	_____ (when)
I went to school in	_____ (place)
at	_____ (type)
My parents came from	_____
After leaving school, I studied	_____ (subject)
at	_____

| **I did** | a degree
a course
an apprenticeship | **in** | _____ (subject) |

After that I	_____
My first job was in	_____
as a(n)	_____
More recently I have been working as	_____ (job)
in	_____ (where)
with	_____ (company)

A fter you have completed this page, check that you remember all the important language by covering one column and recalling the complete sentences. Notice the prepositions. Can you make questions to ask someone else about him- or herself?

A s every business person knows, you don't talk about business all the time. Talking about yourself and your business partner can help to build trust and confidence. But different countries talk about different topics and have different taboo topics. Prepare yourself by thinking about your own attitudes (see pages 147 to 159) and the language you need.

YOUR JOB

2

Complete the following sentences about yourself.

My address is _____

My business number is _____

My extension is _____

I work for _____ (company)

        as a(n) _____ (job)

        in the _____ (department)

I mostly deal with _____ (kind of work)

I am responsible   **for** _____ (...ing form)

        and _____

My job involves a lot of _____ (...ing form)

        and _____

What I like about my job is _____

I've been with the company for _____ (period of time)

        since _____ (point in time)

I've been in my present job for _____

After you have completed the page, check that you remember from time to time by covering one column and recalling the whole sentence. Can you make questions to ask someone else for the same information?

YOUR COMPANY 1

2

Draw an organigram of your company. It should show the main structure of the organisation. Label the different parts of the organisation and the jobs in the organisation. As well as some of the words below, you may need special words used in your company.

division   department   section   unit
marketing   sales   production   finance   R and D   production   personnel
chairman   president   vice-chairman   board of directors   managing director
chief executive   director   manager
assistant   deputy   temporary

YOUR COMPANY 2

2

Complete the right-hand part of this page. Make complete sentences about your company. From time to time, cover one half of the page and recall the complete sentences.

The company is divided into

We employ

Our main branches are in

We have subsidiaries in

The company was founded in

I am mostly concerned with

I am responsible to
                 for

Our parent company is

Apart from ourselves, they are also extensively involved in

The people I am in most frequent contact with are (jobs, not names)

Remember to check that you can say both halves of the sentence naturally — both the information about your own company, and the correct grammar for the first half of each sentence.

YOUR COMPANY 3

2

Complete this table with real information. Make sure you can use all the words in the table to talk about your situation.

Our	main major most important	product(s) services(s) customers clients competitors (export) market(s) domestic suppliers foreign suppliers priorities targets current projects problems	used to be is / are has / have been will be	_____ _____ _____ _____

Write the initials of four people who are important in your work situation. They can be colleagues, clients, contacts in other companies etc. Then write their job, and some of the reasons why you have regular contact with them.

Initials	Job
Reasons	

Initials	Job
Reasons	

Initials	Job
Reasons	

Initials	Job
Reasons	

The language on this and the previous two pages provides a skeleton for talking about a lot of different parts of your daily life.

YOUR PRODUCT

2

Most companies offer a product or service. Write the name in English of three or four of the most important products/services which your organisation makes/offers.

_____

_____

Write here key words you need to **describe** the products/services. Try to choose words which describe the product in different ways: **size, shape, use.**

_____

_____

_____

_____

Very often in business you want to **compare** a product to an earlier product or a product made by a competitor. Write words here which will help you to compare the products/services you have listed above.

_____

_____

You will also want to talk about **advantages** and **disadvantages** of different products. Choose words to help you to do that and list them here.

_____

_____

_____

You may need a dictionary to help you to find the important words on this page. You will find many of the words you have on this page will help you to choose key words for **word families** (Page 96) and **keywords** (Page 58). You need also to check which verbs will be most help to you (Page 138).

YOUR VALUES

2

Language is for talking about more than business and facts. It can also help you to show what you think, believe and value.

Complete the following honestly.

What is most important to you?

	healthy	_____
	successful	_____
TO BE	correct	_____
	happy	_____
	useful	_____
	_____	_____

	time	fun	
	money	friends	
TO HAVE	security		_____
	status		_____
	comfort		_____
	_____		_____

	well	_____
TO DO	with other people	_____
THINGS	your way	_____
	at your own speed	_____
	efficiently	_____
	_____	_____

Later add more expressions which can be used to make sentences with

TO BE, TO HAVE, and TO DO.

From time to time select three items and remind yourself:

It is important to me to be _____ , to have _____ and to do

things _____ because _____

YOUR PHILOSOPHY

Complete each of these sentences. Don't just fill in the spaces quickly. Think about what you might want to say in English one day. Use the page to help you to use language which is really important to you.

Two of my favourite expressions are....

I think I am....

Other people say I am....

For me, success is....

My work is important to me because....

Money is....

For me, knowing English is....

For me, pleasure is....

For me, learning new things is....

The most important thing about my country for me is....

YOUR FAMILY AND FRIENDS

2

Write down here the initials of **five** people you know well. They can be members of your family, friends, colleagues, clients.

Business people don't talk business all the time. Sometimes we talk about ourselves and people we know. If necessary use a dictionary to make sure you know all these words which are used to describe people.

amusing	aggressive	kind	talented	shy
ambitious	serious	calm	cheerful	fussy
stubborn	hard-working	dynamic	talkative	methodical
lively	strong	decisive	indecisive	considerate
untidy	sociable	loyal	moody	enterprising
easy-going	successful	cold	warm	rigid
optimistic	pessimistic	realistic	idealistic	impulsive
bossy	conscientious	quiet	sensitive	emotional
sincere	honest	out-spoken	reliable	hard
astute	bright	single-minded	careless	relaxed

Put the initials of the people you have chosen beside **three** words for each person. Choose words which describe that person.

Underline all the words which you think are positive in one colour. Use a different colour to underline the words you think are negative.

Use the initials of the people you have listed to start some of these sentences. They give you another way of talking about what people are like. Complete the sentences (silently!) with true information.

doesn't find it easy to ....

is (not) very good at ....ing

has difficulty in ....ing

is (not) very interested in ....

spends a lot of time ....ing

never misses a chance to ....

has the habit of ....ing

believes strongly in ....

is (not) very enthusiastic about ......

has no idea how to ....

Y ou will find it easier to remember any new words or expressions if you fix them in your mind by thinking about people you know and associating the words with the people and with qualities that you like and dislike.

INTRODUCTION

There is some language everyone needs, and which is difficult to learn in class. It is the language we use in social situations, when we want to be polite and pleasant to other people.

Social language uses a lot of fixed expressions. Often you can't translate from your own language – you need to learn natural English expressions. This section will help you with all these important areas:

Essential words
Apologies
Saying 'No'
Saying 'Yes'
Active listening
Language problems
'Would'
Eating out
Visitors
Word lobsters

The last pages of the section, which we call word lobsters, give you a special shape to record your own sentences which start with expressions which are very common in social situations. They are introduced on page 41.

3

ESSENTIAL WORDS

3

SAYING THANK YOU

Thank you.

Thank you very much.

Use these if someone does something simple for you. This is for things you normally expect from other people. They are not strong enough for special help.

Thanks a lot. (informal)

I'm very grateful.

It's very kind of you.

For special help, add one of these to the usual expressions listed above.

REQUESTS AND INVITATIONS

Could you......, please.

Would you...for me, please.

Use 'please' at the end of requests for help when the other person will do something for you. Avoid using 'please' in the middle of a sentence.

A black coffee, please.

Please sit down.

Please help yourselves to the coffee.

Use 'please' as the beginning of invitations or suggestions where the other person will do something for themself.

Please don't wait for me.

Please join us this evening.

WHEN YOU ARE LISTENING

Sorry?

Use this word alone if you want the other person to repeat what they said for any reason – you didn't hear properly, you didn't understand, or even, you didn't believe what you heard!

Really?

Use this alone to ask the other person to continue, to give more details. It shows you are involved in the conversation but expect the other person to say more before you comment yourself.

If your English is not very good, these words will help you to take a natural part in a conversation without you having to say very much! If your English is good, it is important to use these words naturally.

APOLOGIES

I'M AFRAID

Match the remarks, and responses. Write your answers in the table below.

1. **Can you ring me this evening.**   a. **Not completely, I'm afraid.**

2. **Could I speak to...please?**   b. **I'm afraid that's impossible.**

3. **Did you remember to send me that fax?** c. **I'm afraid I completely forgot.**

4. **I'd need about 40% discount.**   d. **I'm afraid I can't.**

5. **Are you happy with that suggestion?**   e. **I'm afraid he's out at the moment.**

6. **What about next Tuesday?**   f. **I'm afraid I can't manage next week at all.**

1	2	3	4	5	6

Add **'I'm afraid'** to any response which will seem unhelpful to the other person. Notice, it makes some quite strong negative responses acceptable.

It is not usually used in written English; in writing, use **'unfortunately'** instead.

Often, instead of the single word 'No', it is better to use **'I'm afraid not'** as a negative response.

OTHER APOLOGIES

In British English the easiest general rule is:

Excuse me   **before** you disturb someone.
                 before you try to pass someone.

Sorry!   **after** you have inconvenienced someone.

Excuse me   is only used **after** you have done something in British English after you have coughed, sneezed, etc.

In American English, **'Excuse me'** is used to apologise **after** you have inconvenienced someone else.

SAYING 'NO'

3

It is very important to avoid using 'No' on its own unless you are annoyed. On its own it usually sounds aggressive and unhelpful. There are many other ways of giving a negative response. Match these remarks and responses.

1. Did your Head Office agree?   a. No, not yet.

2. Coffee?   b. I'm afraid I've no idea.

3. What's the code for Birmingham?   c. I'd rather you didn't.

4. Have they confirmed the order yet?   d. Not at the moment, thank you.

5. Do you mind if I arrive a bit late?   e. I'm afraid not.

6. Is 25% all right?   f. Well, I really need a bit more than that.

Collect more ways of saying 'No' naturally. Check by covering the English and recalling the natural English expressions.

1	2	3	4	5	6

YOUR LANGUAGE   ENGLISH

SAYING 'NO'

List expressions used to answer 'No' naturally and pleasantly.

Make sure you know their equivalents in your own language. Check the English from time to time by covering the right hand column.

3

YOUR LANGUAGE	ENGLISH

SAYING 'YES'

There are lots of expressions which are more natural and polite than using the single word 'Yes'. Match these remarks and responses. Notice that the natural expressions are quite different from simple, one-word answers.

1. **Will delivery by the end of the month be all right?**

2. **Could I have another cup of coffee?**

3. **Is it OK to park here?**

4. **Would you like me to copy it for you?**

5. **Can I count on your support?**

6. **Is next Thursday suitable for our next meeting?**

a. **Yes, I think so.**

b. **Yes, please.**

c. **Of course; help yourself.**

d. **Yes, that'll be fine.**

e. **As far as I'm concerned.**

f. **Yes. I'm in complete agreement.**

Write your answers here:

1	2	3	4	5	6

Collect more ways of saying 'Yes' and list them below. Check that you know the natural expressions by covering the English and recalling them.

YOUR LANGUAGE	ENGLISH

SAYING 'YES'

In English you do not usually reply with the single word 'Yes'. One-word replies can sound aggressive or rude. It is natural to answer with a short phrase or sentence.

During your course, listen for these replies. Note them here. Make a list of similar phrases in your own language. Check you have learned the natural English by covering the English and trying to recall the natural language.

3

YOUR LANGUAGE	ENGLISH

ACTIVE LISTENING

3

Different countries have different customs (see page 147) but in many places people who are speaking expect their listener to show interest and involvement. If you listen in complete silence, people may think you are difficult to talk to! Make a list of sounds or expressions which you can use to show you are listening.

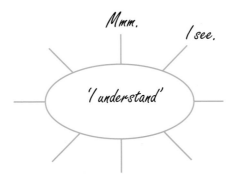

Mmm.

I see.

'I understand'

Make a list of expressions you can use to show you do not understand, or need something repeated or explained.

I don't quite follow.

Sorry. What exactly do you mean?

LANGUAGE PROBLEMS

If you find it difficult to understand natural English conversation you need expressions to help you to control what other people say. Make sure you know how to use all the expressions below.

3

WHEN YOU DON'T UNDERSTAND

Sorry, I'm afraid I don't understand. (at all)

I don't know what......means. (You really don't know.)

I don't know what you mean by...... (You think you must misunderstand)

Just a moment, please. What (exactly) does........mean? (To check)

I didn't catch/follow that (completely). Could you just go over it again?

Could you just repeat that, please? (You want everything repeated.)

Could you just repeat (the figures/the dates/your fax number/...) **please?**

SAYING WHAT YOU NEED

Could I just have a minute, please. (You want a pause to think/write/....)

Could you just say that slowly, so I can make a note, please.

Could you spell (your name/address/company name/....), **please.**

EXPLAINING YOUR LANGUAGE PROBLEMS

I'm afraid I don't know the English word for...... . Can you help me?

I'm afraid I can't explain very clearly in English. (But I'll do my best.)

Have I made myself clear? (Gives the other person chance to check with you.)

I think you must have misunderstood me. (The other person seems annoyed or confused.)

YOU NEED TIME TO REACT

Really? (See page 28)

Can you give a few more details (about.......), **please?**

That's very interesting. It really gives me something to think about.

WOULD 1

REQUESTS

Would you	take a copy of this for me, please.
	ask him to phone please.
	let me know as soon as possible, please.

OFFERS

Would you like us to	fax it for you?
	book a hotel for you?
	call a taxi for you?

| Would you like to | join us for dinner? |
| | phone your office before we start? |

| Would you like | some coffee? |
| | a copy? |

SUGGESTIONS

If I were you, I'd.....(sell now).

PREFERENCES

| Wouldn't it be better to | meet as soon as possible. |
| | come back to this question later? |

| I'd prefer | a soft drink, if you don't mind. |
| | to go by train. |

INTRODUCING A COMMENT

I'd like to	begin by ....
	agree, but ....
	welcome you to ....
	ask if ....
	add that ....
	move on to ....

WOULD 2

WOULD

There are many useful expressions which begin with different phrases that all include **would** or **'d**. List the ones which are most useful for you here.

Would you like
— my secretary to copy it for you?
— somebody to take you to the airport?

Would you
— get back to me as soon as possible, please?
— ring me early next week, after the conference, please?

I'd like to
— thank you all for joining us today.
— begin by welcoming you all.

Remember, if you say the expressions aloud several times, and then say them onto a cassette tape which you listen to later, it will help you to remember and feel comfortable with the new language.

EATING OUT 1

Every professional person knows how important it is to be able to meet colleagues and clients over food or a drink as well as in the office or at meetings. Sometimes this social language is difficult. Here are the most important words and expressions to help you.

Here are some important words you can use as word partnerships with the word **restaurant**. Make sure you know the equivalent in your language

a popular restaurant	**a first class restaurant**
a Chinese restaurant	**a simple Italian restaurant**
a famous Greek restaurant	**an excellent French restaurant**
an interesting seafood restaurant	**a nearby Indian restaurant**

MAKING ARRANGEMENTS

I thought we might go to a........restaurant I know, this evening.

I've booked a table for (eight o'clock) at a........restaurant.

Shall I pick you up at your hotel about (quarter to eight)?

I'll ask........to pick you up about (half past seven).

BEFORE THE MEAL

Would you like a drink to begin with (or shall we order straightaway)?

Can I suggest the............ . It's a local speciality.

They serve very good...........if you like it/them.

CHOOSING

I think I'll have the..........please.

The same for me, please.

DURING THE MEAL

This is very good. How's your........?

Would you like a little more.....?

Oh, thank you./No thanks. I'm fine.

LEAVING

Can we have the bill please.

Do you take VISA/American Express, please.

Could you call us a taxi, please.

EATING OUT 2

Make a list of three or four things to eat or drink which are local specialities which you might suggest a visitor could try. Can you explain them in English? Don't translate, explain. These expressions might help you:

It's/They're a sort of ....

It's/They're a bit like ....

It's got ....**in it.**

It's/They're cooked with ....

Be careful! It's very spicy/strong.

Put your list on the left, and write a full explanation on the right. Check later by covering the explanation to see if you can remember it.

LOCAL SPECIALITY	EXPLANATION IN ENGLISH

VISITORS

The language of the short speeches when we greet visitors or thank people at the end of a visit is very standardised. You can use these on most occasions.

GREETING VISITORS

❝ **Good morning (Ladies and Gentlemen). On behalf of........may I welcome you to........ . It is a great pleasure to have you with us today. I hope you enjoy your visit/meeting/the conference. If there is anything we can do to help, please do not hesitate to ask. Now, you don't want to listen to me all day so I'll hand you over to my colleague ....(who will show you...../take you to......).** ❞

A TOAST WITH VISITORS

❝ **Ladies and Gentlemen, could I just say a few words. It is a great pleasure to have you with us today. We hope you have enjoyed your visit. We are delighted to have had the opportunity to show you......../introduce ....to you/ meet so many of you (personally). We look forward to getting to know you all better/building on our already very successful co-operation/providing you with the service you need. So, let's raise our glasses to our future co-operation.** ❞

THANKING FOR A VISIT

❝ **Could I just say a few words? On behalf of........and myself may I express our warmest thanks for today's visit/the last few days/........ . I'm sure I speak for everyone when I say we have found the visit/meeting/........ very interesting and useful. We are very grateful to everyone who has helped to make our visit/ the meeting so rewarding and enjoyable. (I should particularly like to thank........ who was responsible fo the arrangements.) Thank you very much. We hope we may soon/one day/........ have the pleasure of welcoming (some of) you to............. .** ❞

WORD LOBSTER 1

The first words of some sentences are very common and very important in the language needed by business people. Some of the most important are listed for you. There is also space for you to add your own important examples.

It is very difficult to remember language which is just lists of new words. These special shapes, which we call 'word lobsters' will help you to remember more easily. Fill the 'legs' with useful expressions. Add a translation if you think it helps you. From time to time, cover the right hand part of the page and make sure you can recall the important expressions you have listed.

have a short break, shall we?
come back to that point later.

Let's

we meet again on the 17th?
you ring me again early next week?

May I suggest

T ry to write natural sentences about your own business. These will be more useful and easier to remember.

WORD LOBSTER 2

Fill the important first words of other sentences that you may need to help you to have a natural conversation. Complete the legs of the lobster in the same way as on the previous page. Cover the expressions from time to time to check what you have learned.

3

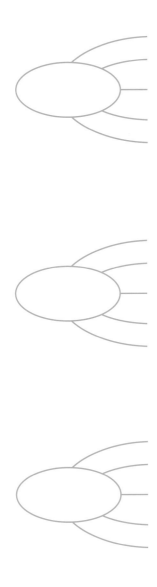

WORD LOBSTER 3

Fill the important first words of other sentences that you may need to help you to have a natural conversation. Complete the legs of the lobster in the same way as on the previous page. Cover the expressions from time to time to check what you have learned.

3

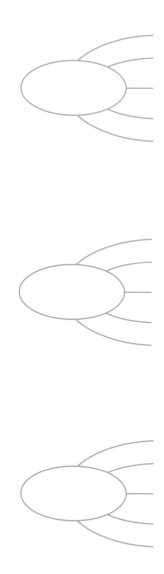

WORD LOBSTER 4

Fill the important first words of other sentences that you may need to help you to have a natural conversation. Complete the legs of the lobster in the same way as on the previous page. Cover the expressions from time to time to check what you have learned.

3

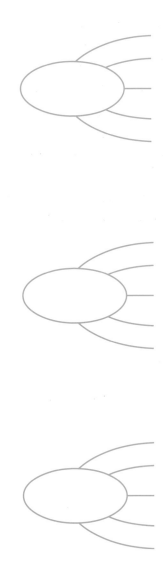

USING PROFESSIONAL TEXTS

One of the most important parts of your professional language course is the part you make yourself with your teacher. You need to select language useful to you from natural professional texts.

Usually you read for information or pleasure. Here you are going to use texts for a completely different purpose — to help you find language you need. You will waste a lot of time if you try to understand every word.

This section of the book will help you to use texts to help your English.

In addition to reading you can also **listen** to natural English regularly. The BBC World Service has many helpful programmes, including the news and programmes of special interest to business people. You can use them in a similar way — as a resource to find language useful to you.

You will find it particularly useful to identify and record word partnerships around certain key words (see pages 57 to 76). Here are some sources of useful professional language texts:

Company brochures	Promotional materials
Product descriptions	Technical manuals
Product samples	Trade journals
In-house newsletters	Adverts
Examples of letters	Taped phone calls
Minutes of meetings	Company reports

You can also use newspapers to find topical business language. Two which are usually easy to get are:

The Financial Times	International Herald Tribune

4

USING HEADLINES 1

Use a newspaper such as the Financial Times. Look through the paper's headlines and other large print. Look for useful two-word partnerships. List the partnerships you find in a two column format. It will help you if you use different lists for different kinds of partnership, for example adjective-noun. Here are some from one issue of a newspaper:

hostile reaction

prime rates

slower sales

political and economic pressures

Green Consumers

Brutal repression

Best Value

List them like this:

ADJECTIVE	NOUN	ADJECTIVE	NOUN
hostile	reaction	prime	rates
brutal	repression	green	consumers
slower	sales	political	pressure(s)
best	value	economic	pressure(s)

After you have made the lists, check regularly if you can remember by covering one column and recalling the words in the other column.

I t will help you to remember the partnerships if you think of a strong image or picture for each one. It also helps if you try to identify some personal meaning for each partnership you record. Take time while you are choosing and recording them. It is an investment of time. You will have the profit when you remember better.

USING HEADLINES 2

Here are some more large print examples from the paper. What kind of words are used to make these word partnerships? These are two more kinds of partnership which you can list in two columns on the following pages. Put headings on the columns below.

outlines the problems

makes the initial decisions

launch campaign

halt negotiations

relieve stress

take a year off

4

....	....
outline	a/the problem
make	a decision

....	....
launch	a campaign
take	a year off

opinion poll

election victory

Sales Personnel

power struggle

Book Trade

CAREER OPPORTUNITIES

....	....
opinion	poll
book	trade

....	....
power	struggle
career	opportunities

USING AN ARTICLE 1

4

Take an article and search through for word partnerships. Remember, you need to choose the article and choose the word partnerships. Most people do not need partnerships like *optical bleaches,* but many more people will use *environmentally friendly, ordinary people, a small percentage.* **Choose the partnerships you think will be useful to you.**

As an example only, how many useful word partnerships can you find in this article? Underline them as you read the article.

Providing environment-friendly goods has great marketing potential as shoppers start to put ecological soundness first

The biggest market opportunities are in the fast-moving consumer-goods area – washing powder, household cleaning supplies, paper products and food – because these are the sort of products that ordinary people have to buy every day.

Last month's launch of a new range of ecologically friendly cleaning products, under the Ark brand name, guided by Bryn Jones, a former Greenpeace director, is a good example of the greening of our supermarket shelves.

What is special about Ark products is that they do not contain phosphates, which can get into rivers and kill fish and plants, nor chlorine bleach, which can produce dioxin, a carcinogenic compound, nor biological enzymes, which have been linked with skin problems.

Will Ark products actually be accepted by the customer as doing the job as well as conventional, non-ecologically sound cleaners? Take whiteness, for example: most washing powders contain so-called optical bleaches, which make clothes look whiter than white.

That is, of course, the crux of the matter: only a small percentage of the public will put ecological soundness above all other considerations when filling a supermarket trolley. Most consumers will put other priorities, such as whiteness, above green-ness.

Yet the indications are that the green consumer movement is growing in strength, especially among mothers with young children – and, let's face it, it is still women who do most of the shopping.

So what kind of products are likely to appeal to the green consumers? Ark has demonstrated that there is a demand for green cleaners, and the success of the Body Shop is clear proof that there is a ready market for green cosmetics.

Parents' concerns over chlorine bleaches used in disposable nappies and other paper products has led to the greening of the nappy. Increasingly, battery manufacturers are describing their products as environmentally friendly. Lead-free petrol is becoming more popular.

The recent concern over contamination of foodstuffs has fuelled an already growing movement towards cleaner, healthier food in our shops.

Anyone who has paused by the organic-food displays in leading supermarkets cannot but be struck by two immediate facts: people are prepared to pay well over the odds for food they believe to be less contaminated with "artificial" fertilizers and pesticides, and, for some reason, the more "organic" the produce is, the more earth seems to be sticking to it.

But reseach shows that the public is not fooled by a label saying "green" on a product, or by a few cosmetic, changes – and Britain's major manufacturers have recognized this.

There is a list on the opposite page.

USING AN ARTICLE 2

Here are some of the partnerships you may have found in the article opposite. You can list them in the usual two-column format, or, if you find three-word partnerships, you can list these by using a mark like this (▼)

4

great		ecologically	friendly
▼ marketing	potential	brand	name
fast-moving	consumer-goods	a small	percentage
washing	powder	put above	
household		▼ other	considerations
▼ cleaning	supplies	appeal to	
ordinary	people	▼ the green	consumer

By listing the word partnerships in this way you can check what you can remember very easily. Can you recall the missing words in these partnerships? — if not, check in the article.

	shelves		petrol
clear		fuelled	
	market		
parents'		pay well	

When you think you have learned some useful combinations, write a short summary of the article (or part of it). Use as many of the partnerships as you can, but without looking at the article or list while you are writing.

Choosing articles which contain word partnerships useful to talk about your business and interests is a very efficient way of improving your English.

VERB - NOUN PARTNERSHIPS

Choose your own texts. Use them in the same way as the text on page 48.
List useful partnerships from the texts you choose here.

VERB	NOUN	VERB	NOUN

4

ADJECTIVE - NOUN PARTNERSHIPS

Choose your own texts. Use them in the same way as the text on page 48.
List useful partnerships from the texts you choose here.

ADJECTIVE	NOUN	ADJECTIVE	NOUN

4

NOUN - NOUN PARTNERSHIPS

Choose your own texts. Use them in the same way as the text on page 48.
List useful partnerships from the texts you choose here.

4

NOUN	NOUN	NOUN	NOUN

USEFUL EXPRESSIONS 1

While you are using texts to find and list useful word partnerships, you will certainly find some useful expressions and idioms as well. It is not as easy to list these in a system, but again we suggest you write them so you can cover part of the expression, or write an equivalent in your own language which you can cover later when you want to check what you have learned. Use the following pages to record useful language. Here are a few expressions to suggest the kind of language you and your teacher can look for together.

4

ENGLISH	YOUR LANGUAGE
worth a look	
across the country	
absolutely free	
hopes and fears	
we are committed to excellence	

USEFUL EXPRESSIONS 2

Use this page to record useful expressions and idioms. Give equivalents in your own language. Check by covering your language, or by covering part of the English expression.

4

ENGLISH

YOUR LANGUAGE

USEFUL EXPRESSIONS 3

Use this page to record useful expressions and idioms. Give equivalents in your own language. Check by covering your language, or by covering part of the English expression.

ENGLISH   YOUR LANGUAGE

4

USEFUL EXPRESSIONS 4

Use this page to record useful expressions and idioms. Give equivalents in your own language. Check by covering your language, or by covering part of the English expression.

4

ENGLISH	YOUR LANGUAGE

KEYWORDS

Several sections of this book help you to identify and record words which often occur together. (The technical name for these is 'collocations'.) If you want to talk about your **car** you will certainly need the word partnerships **buy a new car, park the car, leave the car at home.** From a single **keyword** we can collect and organise the words which are the basic material for many natural sentences. This section

a. presents a group of important keywords for business English and helps you find and record important word partnerships.

b. gives you space to choose your own keywords and find and record their important word partnerships.

5

The keywords presented in this section are:

> **Contract/Agreement**
> **Sales** (These pages show you how to use the section)
> **Price(s)**
> **Costs**
> **Market**
> **Advertising**
> **Production**
> **Product**
> **Company**
> **Department/Office**
> **Order**
> **Offer**
> **Tax(es)**
> **Staff/Personnel**

This is followed by several pages for your own keywords.

KEYWORDS INTRODUCTION 1

Many professional words are regularly used with a small number of other words. Instead of learning individual words you will find it much more useful to learn word partnerships. In the middle of the diagram is a **keyword.** Around it are **background words** of two different kinds. Underline them with two different coloured pens.

5

alter   unworkable   conditional   temporary   modify

discuss

exclusive   sign   break   check   draft   draw up   outline

go over

A CONTRACT
AN AGREEMENT   negotiate   satisfactory

terminate   export   short-term

non-renewable   one-year

trade   sales

legal   renew   licensing   reject   review

In this example you should have:

> **Verbs** which go in front of the keyword: **sign** an agreement.
> Words which go **between** the verb and the keyword: sign a **temporary**/**trade** agreement.

Make a list of word partnerships. Find two-word partnerships
(verb + keyword) or three-word partnerships (verb + adjective/noun + keyword)

_____   _____   _____

_____   _____   _____

Usually on the following pages we then suggest that you write some sentences about your own situation using some of the partnerships. As usual, this will help you remember the partnerships better.

KEYWORDS INTRODUCTION 2

Not all the keywords work in the same way. Sometimes the keyword is at the centre of a word partnership. In the diagram below you need to find words which **follow** the keyword: sales **strategy**, sales **drive.** Underline these in one colour. Now underline verbs which can come **in front of one of the two-word partnerships** you have made: **discuss** sales strategy, **launch** a sales drive.

In these examples the three-word partnerships are often almost complete sentences: **We need to discuss our sales strategy**. Write some more three-word partnerships of this kind.

_____   _____   _____

_____   _____   _____

As usual we will ask you to write sentences about your own situation.

_____

With these word partnerships you can often say a lot without using difficult grammar. Instead of *'How many of these can we sell in America?'* it is quicker, easier and more natural to say *'What's the American sales potential?'*

KEYWORDS 1

The word in the centre of the diagram is the **keyword**. There are different kinds of words in the **background** words. Use different coloured pens to underline the background words so that you divide them into groups. Find some two-word and three-word partnerships. Look for some partnerships which include **the keyword** and **a verb** from the background words. Write four sentences about your own situation. Use coloured pens or highlight the word partnerships so you can check them easily later.

5

alter   unworkable   discuss   conditional   temporary   modify

exclusive   sign   break   check   draft   draw up   outline

go over

A CONTRACT   negotiate   satisfactory

terminate   export   *AN AGREEMENT*   short-term

non-renewable   one-year

trade   sales

legal   renew   licensing   reject   review

_____   _____   _____

_____   _____   _____

_____

_____

_____

_____

KEYWORDS 2

The word in the centre of the diagram is the **keyword**. There are different kinds of words in the **background** words. Use different coloured pens to underline the background words so that you divide them into groups. Find some two-word and three-word partnerships. Look for some partnerships which include **the keyword** and **a verb** from the background words. Write four sentences about your own situation. Use coloured pens or highlight the word partnerships so you can check them easily later.

area   representative   launch   present   volume
                                          forecast   drive

target   increase   discuss   calculate

            maintain   pay   technique
boost   SALES   set   prospect

            figures   meeting
manager   call
                     potential   commission

    assess   win/lose
            fix   reach
adopt   report   quota   extend
            strategy   call on

5

_____   _____   _____

_____   _____   _____

_____

_____

_____

_____

KEYWORDS 3

The word in the centre of the diagram is the **keyword**. There are different kinds of words in the **background** words. Use different coloured pens to underline the background words so that you divide them into groups. Find some two-word and three-word partnerships. Look for some partnerships which include **the keyword** and **a verb** from the background words. Write four sentences about your own situation. Use coloured pens or highlight the word partnerships so you can check them easily later.

5

offer   raise   fix   cash   cut   list   sale

reduce   range   limit   quote

lower   PRICE(S)   sensitivity

reduction   retail   increase   object to

agree   rise   discount

wholesale

_____   _____   _____

_____   _____   _____

_____

_____

_____

KEYWORDS 4

The word in the centre of the diagram is the **keyword**. There are different kinds of words in the **background** words. Use different coloured pens to underline the background words so that you divide them into groups. Find some two-word and three-word partnerships. Look for some partnerships which include **the keyword** and **a verb** from the background words. Write four sentences about your own situation. Use coloured pens or highlight the word partnerships so you can check them easily later.

5

advertising   capital   analyse   unit

cut   overhead

reduce   variable

total

compare   COSTS   production

break down   material

                                           labour

                              bring down

absorb   fixed   indirect   increase

                          direct

spread   average

_____   _____   _____

_____   _____   _____

_____

_____

_____

_____

KEYWORDS 5

The word in the centre of the diagram is the **keyword**. There are different kinds of words in the **background** words. Use different coloured pens to underline the background words so that you divide them into groups. Find some two-word and three-word partnerships. Look for some partnerships which include **the keyword** and **a verb** from the background words. Write four sentences about your own situation. Use coloured pens or highlight the word partnerships so you can check them easily later.

carry out   capture   survey

break into   response

                            analyse

enter   research

open   free   MARKET   seize

increase   buyer's

trends

        move   leader   share   Japanese

                            sector

European

        forces   growing   domestic

KEYWORDS 6

The word in the centre of the diagram is the **keyword**. There are different kinds of words in the **background** words. Use different coloured pens to underline the background words so that you divide them into groups. Find some two-word and three-word partnerships. Look for some partnerships which include **the keyword** and **a verb** from the background words. Write four sentences about your own situation. Use coloured pens or highlight the word partnerships so you can check them easily later.

conduct   campaign   agency

take   national   launch   reduce

prepare   TV   budget   slogan

ADVERTISING

style   rates   press

costs

space   regional   devise   trade

copy

concept   change   appoint

5

KEYWORDS 7

The word in the centre of the diagram is the **keyword**. There are different kinds of words in the **background** words. Use different coloured pens to underline the background words so that you divide them into groups. Find some two-word and three-word partnerships. Look for some partnerships which include **the keyword** and **a verb** from the background words. Write four sentences about your own situation. Use coloured pens or highlight the word partnerships so you can check them easily later.

5

capacity   control   start   train   line
set   system
                                site
        license
            costs   efficient   hold up
halt
      transfer   *PRODUCTION*
                                        engineer
problems   speed   plan

                                                    target
    levels   supervise   maintain   check

overcome   increase   automate

_____   _____   _____

_____   _____   _____

_____

_____

_____

_____

KEYWORDS 8

The word in the centre of the diagram is the **keyword**. There are different kinds of words in the **background** words. Use different coloured pens to underline the background words so that you divide them into groups. Find some two-word and three-word partnerships. Look for some partnerships which include **the keyword** and **a verb** from the background words. Write four sentences about your own situation. Use coloured pens or highlight the word partnerships so you can check them easily later.

sell

new   develop   range   specifications   advertise

promote

manager   modify   **(A/THE) PRODUCT**   design

distribute   features   promotion

demonstrate   improve   manufacture   test

launch   invent

These words can, of course, be used with the name of your particular product instead of the general word 'product'.

_____   _____   _____

_____   _____   _____

_____

_____

_____

_____

KEYWORDS 9

The word in the centre of the diagram is the **keyword**. There are different kinds of words in the **background** words. Use different coloured pens to underline the background words so that you divide them into groups. Find some two-word and three-word partnerships. Look for some partnerships which include **the keyword** and **a verb** from the background words. Write four sentences about your own situation. Use coloured pens or highlight the word partnerships so you can check them easily later.

5

well-run   re-structure   invest in

found   car   register   run

buy into

join   oil   profitable   new

local   A/THE   big

holding   COMPANY   leave

start up   take over

set up

foreign

float   finance   Public   Limited

subsidiary   work for

manage   medium-sized

KEYWORDS 10

The word in the centre of the diagram is the **keyword**. There are different kinds of words in
the **background** words. Use different coloured pens to underline the background words so
that you divide them into groups. Find some two-word and three-word partnerships. Look
for some partnerships which include **the keyword** and **a verb** from the background words.
Write four sentences about your own situation. Use coloured pens or highlight the word
partnerships so you can check them easily later.

5

advertising   complaints   take over

            run   supervise

marketing   be in charge of

        sales   (DEPARTMENT
                        OFFICE)   (be) put in charge of

    head
            finance   join   legal

accounts

        manage   re-structure   production

_____   _____   _____

_____   _____   _____

_____

_____

_____

_____

KEYWORDS 11

The word in the centre of the diagram is the **keyword**. There are different kinds of words in the **background** words. Use different coloured pens to underline the background words so that you divide them into groups. Find some two-word and three-word partnerships. Look for some partnerships which include **the keyword** and **a verb** from the background words. Write four sentences about your own situation. Use coloured pens or highlight the word partnerships so you can check them easily later.

5

phone about

confirm

repeat

win

delay

dispatch

cancel   special

large

supply

fax   lose

£3m

stock

receive

regular

place

(AN)
ORDER

wholesale

check

get

initial

meet

written

bulk

handle

_____   _____   _____   _____

_____   _____   _____   _____

_____

_____

_____

_____

KEYWORDS 12

The word in the centre of the diagram is the **keyword**. There are different kinds of words in the **background** words. Use different coloured pens to underline the background words so that you divide them into groups. Find some two-word and three-word partnerships. Look for some partnerships which include **the keyword** and **a verb** from the background words. Write four sentences about your own situation. Use coloured pens or highlight the word partnerships so you can check them easily later.

detailed

submit   work

revise

provisional   revised

prepare

(AN) OFFER   accept

make   final

receive   withdraw

firm

5

KEYWORDS 13

The word in the centre of the diagram is the **keyword**. There are different kinds of words in the **background** words. Use different coloured pens to underline the background words so that you divide them into groups. Find some two-word and three-word partnerships. Look for some partnerships which include **the keyword** and **a verb** from the background words. Write four sentences about your own situation. Use coloured pens or highlight the word partnerships so you can check them easily later.

5

levy

earnings   value added   capital

payer   close

pay   reduce   cuts

liability   claim

income   TAX(ES)

be liable

bracket   allowance

relief   deduct   lower   return   loophole

avoid   inspector

year   code   consultant

complete

KEYWORDS 14

The word in the centre of the diagram is the **keyword**. There are different kinds of words in the **background** words. Use different coloured pens to underline the background words so that you divide them into groups. Find some two-word and three-word partnerships. Look for some partnerships which include **the keyword** and **a verb** from the background words. Write four sentences about your own situation. Use coloured pens or highlight the word partnerships so you can check them easily later.

5

appoint   white-collar   employ   sales   lose

recruit   hire   (un)skilled

qualified   STAFF   need

trained   PERSONNEL   poach

take on   key   office

well paid   look for

motivate   train   interview

KEYWORDS 15

Now use your own keywords; collect background words by using a dictionary or talking to your teacher. Remember you need to be able to talk about yourself and your interests as well as your work!

KEYWORDS 16

Now use your own keywords; collect background words by using a dictionary or talking to your teacher. Remember you need to be able to talk about yourself and your interests as well as your work!

5

KEYWORDS 17

Now use your own keywords; collect background words by using a dictionary or talking to your teacher. Remember you need to be able to talk about yourself and your interests as well as your work!

INTRODUCTION

"Without grammar you can't say much, without vocabulary you can't say anything." Learning words is important, but learning grammar is important too.

Several sections of this book help you to identify and record the words, and the word partnerships, which will be particularly useful to you.

This section helps you to organise the parts of English grammar which are most important for business English. It helps you to say things accurately and naturally and to avoid mistakes. There are special pages to make a note of the language you need to avoid your own 'favourite' mistakes!

This is the largest section of the book and there are several separate sub-sections. These are:

General Business Grammar	The basic grammar to make a sentence more natural/diplomatic.
Being Diplomatic	Space to record important natural expressions.
Grammar of Change	How to talk about trends, graphs, increase/decrease etc.
Word Families	Keywords which have different forms and make important word partnerships. Space to make your own.
Business Verbs	Important verbs for talking about business conversations/discussions.
Have	Word partnerships with this key verb.
Two-word Verbs	These are a very important part of natural spoken English. Identify and record the most useful for you.
Business Prepositions	
Business Prefixes	
Important Mistakes	Space to record the correct English so you can avoid **your** mistakes.
Word Contrasts	More space to help you avoid mistakes.
Possibility and Neccessity	Ways to avoid unnatural English.
Your Work Situation	Verb forms needed to talk about yourself.

6

GENERAL BUSINESS GRAMMAR 1

There are some general remarks we can make about the language used to discuss and negotiate effectively in business. Usually we try to avoid sounding dogmatic or inflexible. Usually we hope to find a course of action which suits both parties. English grammar has special ways of doing this. The most general are given here. Notice them when you listen; use them when you present your own ideas. They will make your English more natural and more effective.

INTRODUCTORY PHRASES

Often we introduce our reaction with a word or phrase which tells the listener what kind of comment we are going to make. In particular some phrases warn the listener that disagreement follows. Here are the most common introductory phrases. Which ones are warnings?

Actually,	**With respect,**	**In those circumstances,**
Well,	**To be honest,**	**In fact,**
Frankly,	**As a matter of fact,**	**To put it bluntly,**

WOULD

Would is often added to make any statement more tentative. It takes away the dogmatic tone of many statements.

That is unacceptable.   **That would be unacceptable.**
That does not meet our requirements.   **That would not meet our requirements.**
We need further reassurance.   **We would need further reassurance.**

How could you make these more tentative?

1. That is too late.
2. I prefer to meet before that.
3. We expect them to accept our proposals.
4. We hope to be able to complete soon.
5. Flying has definite advantages.
6. I'm not able to give a guarantee at this stage.
7. Finance is no problem.
8. I'm afraid I don't accept that.

Write some examples of your own here:

_____

_____

_____

_____

GENERAL BUSINESS GRAMMAR 2

SUGGESTIONS

Often suggestions are presented in question form:

| That is too late. | → | **Is that too late?** |
| That would be too late. | → | **Would that be too late?** |

How could these be made more tentative?

30% is too much.
Friday would be convenient.
We need another meeting fairly soon.
We could ask the UN to finance the project.
It would be a good idea to involve the French.
We could cancel.
We've got to increase our offer.
They can raise some of the finance themselves.

The examples above all sound even more tentative and open to negotiation if they are grammatically negative:

Isn't that too late?
Wouldn't that be too late?

Can you change the other examples in the same way.

Write some examples useful in your job here:

_____

_____

_____

_____

_____

_____

_____

_____

6

GENERAL BUSINESS GRAMMAR 3

QUALIFIERS

Successful meetings often depend on avoiding direct disagreement. The more general the statement, the more likely it is to produce disagreement. Not surprisingly, therefore, good negotiators often restrict general statements by using qualifiers. Here are some of the most common qualifiers English:

a **slight** misunderstanding	a **short** delay
a **little bit too** early	a **bit of a** problem
some reservations	a **little** more time

AVOIDING NEGATIVE WORDS

Often English avoids negative adjectives, preferring *not* + positive equivalent:

The hotel was dirty.　➔　**The hotel wasn't very clean.**
The food was cold.　➔　**The food was not very hot.**

Negative words used directly [*It was unacceptable*] are usually **very** negative.

COMPARATIVES

In offering an alternative suggestion, the comparative is often used:

Wouldn't the 31st be more convenient? It might be cheaper to go by air.

The implication is that the other person's suggestion is acceptable, but yours is **more** acceptable. For this reason the use of the comparative is more tactful.

This is not only true for adjectives. Notice these expressions. Each one contains an expression based on the comparative:

There's more chance of them accepting if we ....
I still think they are more likely to agree if ....
We need more information before we agree to anything.

The language points discussed here are general features of English. The features in English may be very different from your own language. It is up to you to decide if you want to use all of the language points discussed here. It is essential, however, if you are going to use English in meetings with native speakers, that you are aware of the way they use English to make their message more direct, more tactful, more diplomatic etc.

6

BEING DIPLOMATIC 1

Use this page to record the natural way to say things diplomatically. Write and record your answers after you have checked with your teacher. Use the lower part of the page for your own examples, about your own job.

_____

(That's inconvenient. I don't want to meet so soon.)

_____

(We have had problems with our distributor.)

_____

(I can't accept such a long delay.)

_____

(That suggestion is useless!)

_____

(That's an unhelpful way of looking at the problem.)

_____

_____

_____

_____

_____

_____

_____

BEING DIPLOMATIC 2

Use this page to record the natural way to say things diplomatically. Write and record your answers after you have checked with your teacher. Use the lower part of the page for your own examples, about your own job.

_____

(The last quarter's sales figures were bad.)

_____

(Next Tuesday is inconvenient.)

_____

(That's a negative attitude!)

_____

(I refuse to believe that!)

_____

(That leaves me with a problem!)

_____

_____

_____

_____

_____

_____

_____

BEING DIPLOMATIC 3

Use this page to record the natural way to say things diplomatically. Write and record your answers after you have checked with your teacher. Use the lower part of the page for your own examples, about your own job.

_____

(They are a bad risk.)

_____

(It's a good idea to take a long-term view.)

_____

(It's dangerous to delay the decision too long.)

6

_____

(That's impossible!)

_____

(That's a stupid idea!)

_____

_____

_____

_____

_____

_____

Could you use very direct language in your language? Does the English seem strange? Do you think there could be problems in international discussions because languages are used differently in different countries? (See pages 150, 151, 159).

GRAMMAR OF CHANGE 1

IMPORTANT WORDS

Sentences like these are very common in business:

WORD PARTNERSHIP	'CHANGE' VERB	'HOW' WORD	WHEN, WHY ETC.
Oil prices	slumped	dramatically	last year.
Production costs	have risen	steadily	as a result of the budget.
Business confidence	will increase	sharply	if the dollar falls.

In business we often want to talk about changes or trends. It is easy to see that all the above sentences could be drawn as graphs. This section will help you with the language we use to put graphs into words.

The most important words are the 'change' verbs. Which of these are about an increase (↑), which about a decrease (↓) and which about staying the same (→)?

Mark the verb with the correct symbol.

rise	go up	peak
grow	increase	jump
come down	level off	decrease
fall	slump	decline
rocket	bottom out	improve
shrink	remain steady	hold firm

You can talk more effectively about changes if you also use a word to describe how the change happened:

slightly	_____	sharply	_____
suddenly	_____	steadily	_____
dramatically	_____	gradually	_____
slowly	_____	immediately	_____

Make sure you can use all these words. Check with a dictionary if necessary. Make sure you know the differences between the 'how' words. Write equivalents in your own language if you think it will help.

GRAMMAR OF CHANGE 2

SENTENCE PATTERN

Here are some basic 'change' words. Complete the other diagrams.

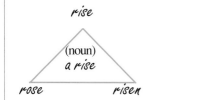 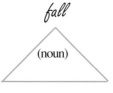 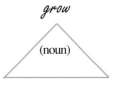

Think of a sentence to describe this graph. Write it down.

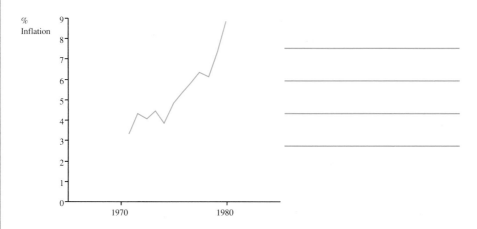

Compare your sentence with these:

Between 1970 and 1980 inflation rose **from** 4% **to** 9% (rose **by** 5%)
Inflation rose **by** 5% **between** 1970 and 1980. is an alternative
Notice the word order

              Time — Subject — Trend
or, sometimes   **Subject — Trend — Time**

Notice these two pattern sentences. Look particularly at the prepositions and the order of the different parts of the sentence.

Sales rose steadily by 200 units from 100 to 300 in the first quarter.

There was a steady rise in sales of 200 units in the first quarter.

The following pages will help you to use the language we need to talk about graphs accurately.

GRAMMAR OF CHANGE 3

VERB FORMS 1

Different forms of the verb have different meanings. Each one has certain time expressions that often occur with it. Here are some of the most useful. There is a short explanation of the verb form and some typical time expressions. All the sentences are ways of talking about the information which is given in the graphs.

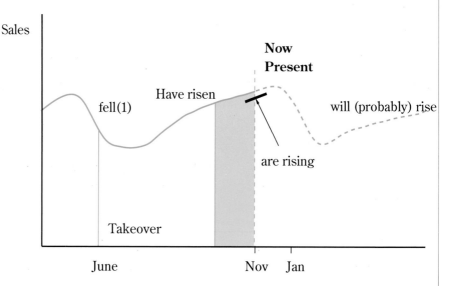

Sales *had fallen* **before the take-over last year.**
Sales *had been falling* **before the take-over last year.**

These verb forms **look back** on something in the past **from an important point in the past.**

Sales *have risen* **in the last few months.**(1)
Sales *have risen* **since the take-over in June.**(2)
Sales *have been rising* **so we are quite pleased.**(3)

This verb form **looks back from the present.** Sometimes you just look back (3); sometimes you give the **period** you are looking back over (1); and sometimes you give the **point** that you look back to (2), when the change began.

Sales *fell* **in the summer.**
Sales *fell* **sharply before the take-over.**

This verb form talks about something in the past, not connected to the present. Sentences like this **always have a time expression** to say exactly when in the past.

GRAMMAR OF CHANGE 4

VERB FORMS 2

Sales *are rising.*

This verb form always refers to the situation **around the present.** It describes a situation which started before the present and one the speaker thinks will continue for at least some time into the future.

Sales *will probably fall* in the New Year.
Sales *will almost certainly* level off next year.

This verb form refers to the future. It is not used for something in the future which is **absolutely** certain, so it is often used with words which say **how** certain the speaker is. Common ones are **probably, possibly, almost certainly, definitely.** The last means "as certain as we can be about the future".

Sales *rise* in the summer and *fall* in the autumn.

This form is used to talk about what is **usually** or **generally** true. It is not used for a trend, but for **a (regular) pattern**. There is no example of this on the graphs opposite, but it can describe, for example, the regular annual pattern found in many businesses.

TALKING ABOUT THE PRESENT SITUATION

Most often in business we want to talk about the situation now. This means two verb forms are particularly important:

AROUND NOW	UP TO NOW
Labour costs **are increasing** and our export customers are starting to complain. (The present continuous)	Our prices **have increased** recently and our customers have started to complain. (The present perfect)

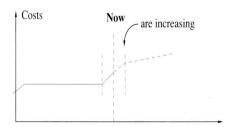

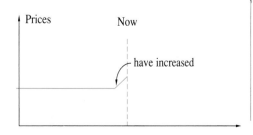

GRAMMAR OF CHANGE 5

PREPOSITIONS 1

List the time expressions which can be used with these prepositions. Notice the verb forms which are used frequently with the expressions you record. All these prepositions are often used with 'change' verbs.

6

SINCE +point

Prices have risen...

since the middle of 1990

FOR +period

Prices have fallen.....
Prices fell.....
Prices will rise....

for longer than we expected

OVER +period

Prices have risen....
Prices rose....
Prices will rise......

over the last/next few months

DURING +period

Prices rose....
Prices have risen......
Prices are rising......
Prices will rise......

during the pre-election period

GRAMMAR OF CHANGE 6

PREPOSITIONS 2

List the time expressions which can be used with these prepositions. Notice the verb forms which are used frequently with the expressions you record. All these prepositions are often used with 'change' verbs.

BY + point

Prices rose......
Prices had risen......
Prices will have risen....

by the end of the (financial) year

AT + point

Prices rose.....
Prices will rise.....

at the beginning/end of (July)

IN +period

Prices rose....
Prices have risen......
Prices will rise......

in the first/last three months of the year

ON +period

Prices rose....
Prices will rise......

on the first of January

6

GRAMMAR OF CHANGE 7

EXPRESSIONS OF TIME

Here is a list of expressions of time. It includes many useful ones, but you can add many more.

The most important difference is between **periods** and expressions which are used as **points** in time. Some of the expressions in this list can be used as both:

> We reduced our staff by 12% **during last year.** (period)
> We have reduced our staff by 12% **since last year.** (point)

Use the two columns to sort the expressions we have given and then add more of your own.

1992

two o'clock

October

the afternoon

the summer

the beginning | of
end

last | weekend
next | month
year

the | last | quarter
next | few months
half-year

PERIODS		POINTS	
_____	_____	_____	_____
_____	_____	_____	_____
_____	_____	_____	_____
_____	_____	_____	_____
_____	_____	_____	_____
_____	_____	_____	_____
_____	_____	_____	_____
_____	_____	_____	_____

GRAMMAR OF CHANGE 8

PREPOSITIONAL PHRASES

In addition to the usual English prepositions (**in, on, at,** etc.) there are a number of preposition phrases made of more than one word. Some of these are important in professional English. Make sure you know the equivalent of each of these in your own language.

ENGLISH	YOUR LANGUAGE	ENGLISH	YOUR LANGUAGE
as a result of . . .		apart from . . .	
because of . . .		due to . . .	
except for . . .		in line with . . .	
in spite of . . .		in the face of . . .	
in view of . . .		on top of . . .	
regardless of . . .		with reference to . . .	

Use some of the expressions above to write about trends in your own situation. Choose 'change' verbs and prepositions from the previous pages.

GRAMMAR OF CHANGE 9

SPECIAL EXPRESSIONS 1

Read this article about inflation in Britain. Some expressions of time have already been underlined. Underline all the others that you find. Make sure you include the preposition that goes with each expression. Then read the article again, looking for expressions of increase (↑) and decrease (↓). Record some of the expressions on the opposite page. Add more expressions from other articles of your own. Use the expressions to talk about your own situation or graphs from articles or reports.

UK inflation hits post-1982 high

Inflation accelerated again last month to the highest level since 1982. Worse for the Chancellor is the fact that there are clear signs that it has yet to peak, and increases can be expected for several months to come.

The markets had expected a slight slow-down, but contrary to expectations yesterday's figures showed a 1.8% jump in the retail price index between March and April.

Housing costs, including rent and rates, and higher charges for gas and electricity accounted for about half the rise. An unexpectedly sharp rise in the price of petrol edged the year-on-year rate up from 7.9% in March to 8% last month.

The news is acutely embarrassing for the Government. The Chancellor has always made it clear that he expects his economic policy to be judged by its success in curbing inflation.

The figure, which is more than double the European average, provided ammunition for Mr Neil Kinnock.

"The year-on-year figure should have started to fall this month. The fact that it hasn't shows the extent of the mess that the government has made of its policies" he said.

RPI

change over previous year

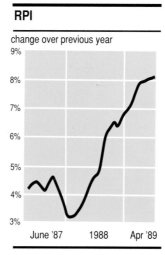

The latest rise brings inflation already to the peak forecast by Mr Lawson in his budget speech less than three months ago. Latest figures suggest further steady rises for some time before modest falls towards the end of the year.

Leading city analysts now seriously doubt whether there is any hope remaining of achieving the 5.5% annual rate forecast by the Chancellor in the Budget for the last quarter of the year. It is now thought that the annual rate could well exceed 7% at the end of the year after peaking at 8.5, or even 9%.

The underlying figures, excluding mortgage interest, also rose. In April last year the figure stood at 4.2%, but it had risen to 5.7% by March, it is now 5.9%.

The Government must be concerned as further price increases are already in the pipeline. Milk and travelling costs have just risen, and petrol has increased by a further 8 to 10 pence a gallon.

The RPI (base Jan. 87 100) rose to 114.3 from the March figure of 112.3.

GRAMMAR OF CHANGE 10

SPECIAL EXPRESSIONS 2

Record useful expressions for increase (↑) and decrease (↓) from the article opposite and other articles which you choose.

NOUN EXPRESSIONS	VERB EXPRESSIONS
a 1.8% jump	*accelerated*
a slight slowdown	*(should have) started to fall*

6

GRAMMAR OF CHANGE 11

COMPANY TRENDS

Describe economic trends in your company using some of the words below as the first words of your sentences. Try to use the change verbs and prepositions from the previous pages.

training	sales	costs	profits
exports	productivity	investment	morale
recruitment	turnover	wages/salaries	market share

Write true sentences about your present situation.

6

GRAMMAR OF CHANGE 12

NATIONAL TRENDS

Describe economic trends in your country using some of the words below as the first words of your sentences. Try to use the change verbs and prepositions from the previous pages.

taxes	earnings	crime	public spending
inflation	poverty	exports	quality of life
imports	interest rates	unemployment	the trade balance

Write true sentences about your present situation.

6

WORD FAMILIES 1

Some important professional words have a whole family of words which are related grammatically. Put one word in the centre and try to find four grammatically related words. You will only find a useful family if you have **at least one verb** and **one noun.** Often there will also be an adjective and one or more extra nouns.

Put the words at the end of the 'arms' of the diagram. Underline the part of the word which is most strongly stressed.

Add words which often make word partnerships with each member of the family.

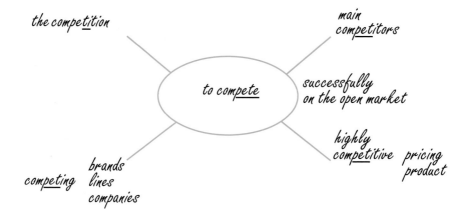

Write sentences about your own situation using different members of the word family.

_____

_____

_____

_____

_____

_____

_____

_____

_____

WORD FAMILIES 2

Some important professional words have a whole family of words which are related grammatically. Put one word in the centre and try to find four grammatically related words. You will only find a useful family if you have **at least one verb** and **one noun.** Often there will also be an adjective and one or more extra nouns.

Put the words at the end of the 'arms' of the diagram. Underline the part of the word which is most strongly stressed.

Add words which often make word partnerships with each member of the family.

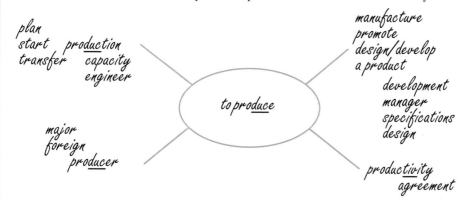

Write sentences about your own situation using different members of the word family.

WORD FAMILIES 3

Some important professional words have a whole family of words which are related grammatically. Put one word in the centre and try to find four grammatically related words. You will only find a useful family if you have **at least one verb** and **one noun.** Often there will also be an adjective and one or more extra nouns.

Put the words at the end of the 'arms' of the diagram. Underline the part of the word which is most strongly stressed.

Add words which often make word partnerships with each member of the family.

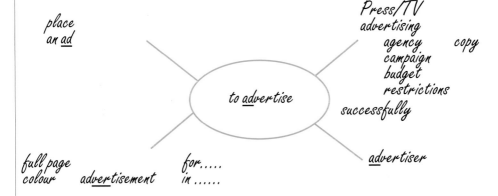

place
an <u>ad</u>

Press/TV
advertising
agency   *copy*
campaign
budget
restrictions
successfully

to <u>ad</u>vertise

full page
colour   *adv<u>er</u>tisement*

for.....
in ......

advert<u>is</u>er

Write sentences about your own situation using different members of the word family.

_____

_____

_____

_____

_____

_____

_____

_____

_____

6

WORD FAMILIES 4

Some important professional words have a whole family of words which are related grammatically. Put one word in the centre and try to find four grammatically related words. You will only find a useful family if you have **at least one verb** and **one noun.** Often there will also be an adjective and one or more extra nouns.

Put the words at the end of the 'arms' of the diagram. Underline the part of the word which is most strongly stressed.

Add words which often make word partnerships with each member of the family.

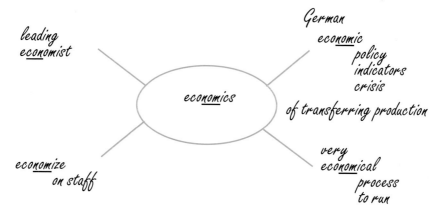

leading
econ<u>o</u>mist

German
econ<u>o</u>mic
policy
indicators
crisis

economics

of transferring production

econ<u>o</u>mize
on staff

very
econ<u>o</u>mical
process
to run

Write sentences about your own situation using different members of the word family.

_____

_____

_____

_____

_____

_____

_____

_____

WORD FAMILIES 5

Some important professional words have a whole family of words which are related grammatically. Put one word in the centre and try to find four grammatically related words. You will only find a useful family if you have **at least one verb** and **one noun.** Often there will also be an adjective and one or more extra nouns.

Put the words at the end of the 'arms' of the diagram. Underline the part of the word which is most strongly stressed.

Add words which often make word partnerships with each member of the family.

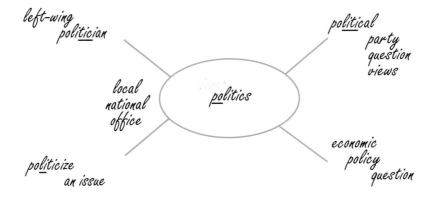

Write sentences about your own situation using different members of the word family.

WORD FAMILIES 6

Some important professional words have a whole family of words which are related grammatically. Put one word in the centre and try to find four grammatically related words. You will only find a useful family if you have **at least one verb** and **one noun.** Often there will also be an adjective and one or more extra nouns.

Put the words at the end of the 'arms' of the diagram. Underline the part of the word which is most strongly stressed.

Add words which often make word partnerships with each member of the family.

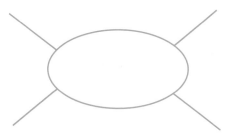

Write sentences about your own situation using different members of the word family.

_____

_____

_____

_____

_____

_____

_____

_____

WORD FAMILIES 7

Some important professional words have a whole family of words which are related grammatically. Put one word in the centre and try to find four grammatically related words. You will only find a useful family if you have **at least one verb** and **one noun.** Often there will also be an adjective and one or more extra nouns.

Put the words at the end of the 'arms' of the diagram. Underline the part of the word which is most strongly stressed.

Add words which often make word partnerships with each member of the family.

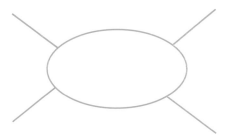

Write sentences about your own situation using different members of the word family.

_____

_____

_____

_____

_____

_____

_____

_____

WORD FAMILIES 8

Some important professional words have a whole family of words which are related grammatically. Put one word in the centre and try to find four grammatically related words. You will only find a useful family if you have **at least one verb** and **one noun.** Often there will also be an adjective and one or more extra nouns.

Put the words at the end of the 'arms' of the diagram. Underline the part of the word which is most strongly stressed.

Add words which often make word partnerships with each member of the family.

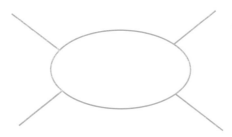

Write sentences about your own situation using different members of the word family.

Remember it will help you to feel comfortable using new language if you record it on cassette tape and listen to yourself saying the new language from time to time.

BUSINESS VERBS 1

Very often in business discussions you will need verbs to talk about communication, words like **ask, agree, advise.**

If you do not want to make unnecessary mistakes you need to know which words and structures can follow these verbs. You can list these in two columns, for example:

ASK	someone for something
	someone to do something
	someone if....
	someone when/how/why....

Use a business dictionary to check how the verbs listed on these pages are used. List in two columns. Write personal examples to make the meaning clear and memorable. Remember to write some questions as well as statements. Later cover one column and try to remember all the combinations in the other column.

It is easier to list the structures if you use:

SO. to mean **someone.** You can put in any name, company etc.

STH. to mean **something.** You **must** put in a noun.

From time to time recall a recent meeting, discussion or phone call. Imagine you are reporting it to someone else. Use some of the verbs on these four pages to describe your conversation.

ACCEPT	STH. (AN offer)	We accepted their revised offer immediately.
	THAT	We accepted that our marketing was not very strong in Spain.
	SO. FOR STH.	We accepted him for the sales reps. job.
ADVISE		
AGREE		

BUSINESS VERBS 2

Continue your list of important communication verbs. Look back often to check what you have recorded.

CONFIRM

CONSIDER

EXPLAIN

INVITE

OBJECT

OFFER

ORDER

6

BUSINESS VERBS 3

Continue your list of important communication verbs. Look back often to check what you have recorded.

6

POINT OUT

PROPOSE

QUERY

RECOMMEND

REFUSE

REJECT

REMIND

BUSINESS VERBS 4

Continue your list of important communication verbs. Look back often to check what you have recorded.

REPLY

RESPOND

SAY

SPEAK

TALK

TELL

WONDER

6

HAVE 1

One of the most important verbs in English is 'have'. It is used in many special expressions. List useful expressions you notice on the key-word diagrams. Write example sentences for the most important examples for you.

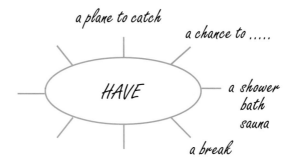

EXAMPLE SENTENCES

_____

_____

_____

_____

_____

_____

_____

_____

_____

_____

_____

_____

_____

_____

HAVE 2

Complete the key-word diagram and write personal example sentences.

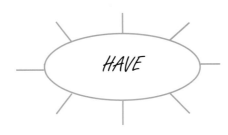

6

EXAMPLE SENTENCES

_____

_____

_____

_____

_____

_____

_____

_____

_____

Note that British and American English are often different here. Many of the things you 'have' in British English (a shower, a break) you 'take' in American English. Listen for examples when you are talking to native speakers of British or American English.

TWO-WORD VERBS 1

English has a lot of two-word verbs. They are very important in natural spoken English. List important verb-preposition combinations in the four columns below and opposite. Test yourself by covering different parts of the tables and recalling the covered words.

You will find it helpful to use a business dictionary to find combinations using these verbs:

BRING, BUY, CARRY, CATCH, DEAL, GET, GIVE, GO, HOLD, KEEP, MAKE, PAY, PULL, PUT, RUN, SELL, SET, TAKE, TURN.

BASIC VERB	PREPOSITION	WORD PARTNERSHIP	MEANING (English/Your language)
back	up	an argument	support
back	out of	an agreement	withdraw from
break	into	a market	penetrate
break	off	negotiations	halt/stop
break	up	a company	separate into parts

6

TWO-WORD VERBS 2

BASIC VERB	PREPOSITION	WORD PARTNERSHIP	MEANING (English/Your language)

6

TWO-WORD VERBS 3

On the previous two pages was one helpful way to list and revise these words which are very important, particularly in spoken English. On this page, put either a **verb** in the centre and add partnerships on the arms (*break off, break up...*) or put the small word in the centre and different verbs on the arms (*pick up, step up...*).

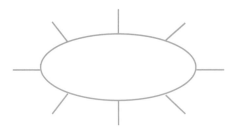

Write useful word partnerships and example sentences.

_____

_____

_____

_____

_____

_____

_____

_____

_____

_____

_____

_____

TWO-WORD VERBS 4

On the earlier pages (110/111) was one helpful way to list and revise these words which are very important, particularly in spoken English. On this page, put either a **verb** in the centre and add partnerships on the arms (*break off, break up*...) or put the small word in the centre and different verbs on the arms (*pick up, step up*...).

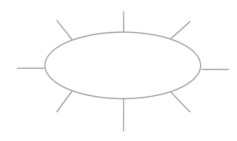

6

Write useful word partnerships and example sentences.

_____

_____

_____

_____

_____

_____

_____

_____

_____

_____

_____

_____

TWO-WORD VERBS 5

On the earlier pages (110/111) was one helpful way to list and revise these words which are very important, particularly in spoken English. On this page, put either a **verb** in the centre and add partnerships on the arms (*break off, break up*...) or put the small word in the centre and different verbs on the arms (*pick up, step up*...).

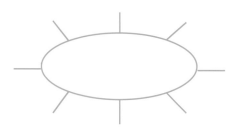

Write useful word partnerships and example sentences.

_____

_____

_____

_____

_____

_____

_____

_____

_____

_____

_____

_____

_____

TWO-WORD VERBS 6

On the earlier pages (110/111) was one helpful way to list and revise these words which are very important, particularly in spoken English. On this page, put either a **verb** in the centre and add partnerships on the arms (*break off, break up...*) or put the small word in the centre and different verbs on the arms (*pick up, step up...*).

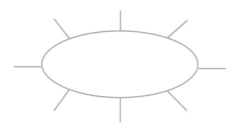

Write useful word partnerships and example sentences.

_____

_____

_____

_____

_____

_____

_____

_____

_____

_____

_____

_____

_____

6

BUSINESS PREPOSITIONS 1

Use these key-word diagrams to list useful examples of words which follow particular prepositions.

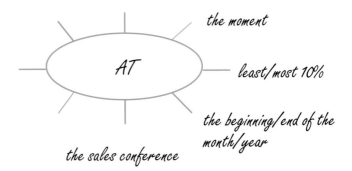

the moment

AT

least/most 10%

the beginning/end of the month/year

the sales conference

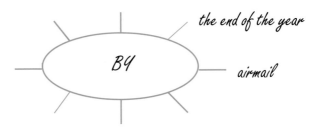

the end of the year

BY

airmail

BUSINESS PREPOSITIONS 2

Complete these key-word diagrams to list words which follow the preposition.

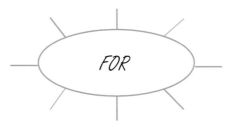

6

BUSINESS PREFIXES 1

A very convenient way to make extra use of some of the words you already know is to add to their meaning with a prefix. Complete the key-word diagram, then write sentences about your own situation.

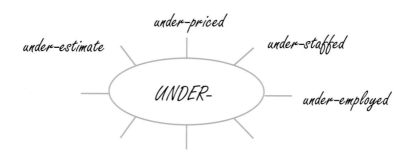

6

EXAMPLE SENTENCES

_____

_____

_____

_____

_____

_____

_____

BUSINESS PREFIXES 2

Complete the key-word diagram, then write sentences about your own situation.

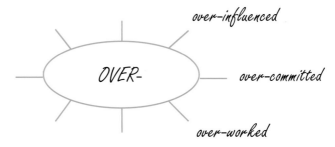

6

EXAMPLE SENTENCES

_____

_____

_____

_____

_____

_____

_____

_____

IMPORTANT MISTAKES 1

Not all mistakes are important. The most important ones are:

> if someone will misunderstand you
> if you give the wrong impression, for example, by sounding rude
> your typical mistakes—things you often get wrong.

Make a list of your important mistakes on these two pages. Cross out the wrong language. From time to time, cover the right hand column, and check that you can remember the correct English.

WRONG	CORRECT
I saw him ~~to~~ go.	I saw him go.
~~I have no possibility to come.~~	I'm afraid I won't be able to come.

IMPORTANT MISTAKES 2

WRONG	CORRECT

6

IMPORTANT MISTAKES 3

Businesses need accounts and so do people learning languages. Accountants use pages divided into columns to record and analyse figures. We suggest you do the same with common mistakes. Many mistakes occur when you make an 'impossible' combination of words. They are another example of the importance of word partnerships. Often 'correcting' a mistake means choosing a good word partnership instead of an impossible one. Look at these examples. In each one, underline a word combination which you think is wrong:

> *We discussed about the meeting.*

> *I told to them the results.*

> *I am staying on the Hilton.*

> *I have been in the company since two years.*

> *Can you explain me why?*

> *Prices are higher in England as in Germany.*

Each 'mistake' is an 'impossible' combination of words. You can list the correct form in two columns like this:

DISCUSS	STH. (WITH SO.)
TELL	SO. STH.
STAY	AT (a hotel) WITH (a family)
SINCE	(A POINT IN TIME) 1987/I left college/the war.
EXPLAIN	TO SO. why/when/how....

This table shows you the type of word which usually follows a particular word. Cover the right hand column and check yourself by making sentences with the words on the left, remembering the type of word which follows. In this way you can make your own grammar practice, and help avoid your most frequent mistakes.

L ist the correct partnerships you need, based on your frequent mistakes on the opposite page. Then check by covering the words in the right hand columns.

IMPORTANT MISTAKES 4

List the correct partnerships you often need here, using the two column system explained opposite.

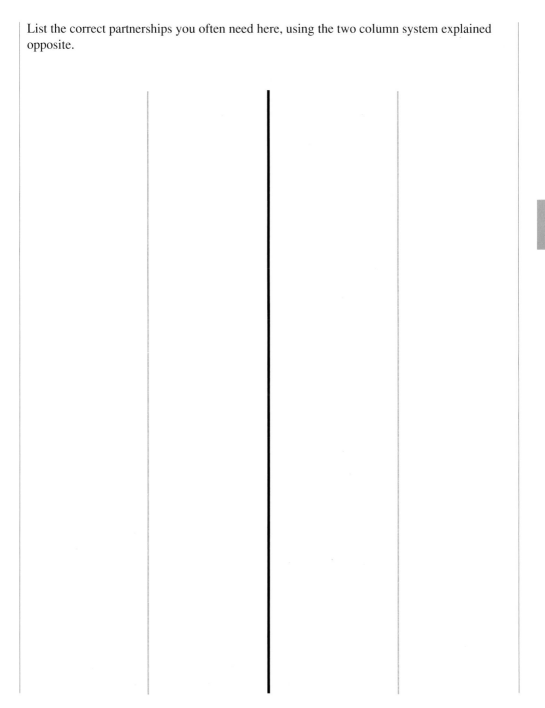

6

WORD CONTRASTS 1

Many typical mistakes happen when you confuse one word or phrase with another. These can be 'false friends' (a word in your language is similar to the wrong English word), or two English words which are similar but used in different ways. On the following pages you will find some important word contrasts. Write two sentences for each pair, showing the correct use of each word. Write one above the line, and one below it. Check your examples are correct if you are unsure. Use the blanks to record other important word contrasts of your own in the same way. Check by covering the right-hand column and recalling the correct examples.

6

THERE
THEY'RE

THERE
THEIR

WILL
WANT

I LIKE
I'D LIKE

WORD CONTRASTS 2

Write two correct sentences, one above and one below the line. Use the blanks to do the same for your own word contrasts.

SAID

TOLD

_____

OFFER

INVITE

_____

LIVE

STAY

_____

_____

_____

_____

6

WORD CONTRASTS 3

Write two correct sentences, one above and one below the line. Use the blanks to do the same for your own word contrasts.

POSSIBILITY AND NECESSITY

We often need to talk about what is possible or necessary, but in English these words are not very common. We use other words, called modal auxiliaries, to talk about these ideas.

The sentences on the left are unusual or unnatural. Match each sentence with one of the sentences on the right.

1. It's possible for him to go.

2. It's not possible for him to go.

3. It wasn't possible for him to go.

4. It's not necessary for him to go.

5. It's necessary for him to go.

6. It's possible that he went.

7. It's possible that he didn't go.

8. It's not possible that he went.

9. It's a good thing for him to go.

10. It's a bad thing for him to go.

11. It's certain that he went.

12. It was possible for him to go and he went.

a. **He can't go.**

b. **He may go.**

c. **He has to go.**

d. **He should go.**

e. **He needn't go.**

f. **He was able to go.**

g. **He couldn't go.**

h. **He shouldn't go.**

i. **He must have gone.**

j. **He can't have gone.**

k. **He may not have gone.**

l. **He may have gone.**

6

Write your answers in this table:

1	2	3	4	5	6	7	8	9	10	11	12

Remember to check later by covering the right hand column. Make sure you can say all the sentences in the right hand column naturally.

YOUR WORK SITUATION

ACCOMPLISHMENTS

| I
We
(Your company) | have | started
finished
succeeded in
decided to
arranged to
agreed to | _____
_____
_____
_____
_____
_____ |

CURRENT ACTIVITIES

| I am
We are | considering
planning
discussing
preparing
.... | _____
_____
_____
_____
_____ |

CURRENT ARRANGEMENTS

| I am
We are | seeing
meeting
going to
launching
.... | _____
_____
_____
_____
_____ |

(Say *when* in each case)

UNREALISED PLANS

| I
We
The company | was
were

could have
should have | going to | _____
_____
_____
_____
_____ | but | _____
_____
_____
_____
_____ |

Notice that each form of the verb has a particular use to describe certain situations in business English.

Check later by covering part of the page and recalling the whole sentences.

INTRODUCTION

Every professional has different language needs, but it is possible to identify some language which is useful to most professional people. In this section you will find that language arranged so it is easy for you to find what you need. It is also easy to add some words of your own so that you can make this professional language useful for you personally.

This section contains the following:

Giving a presentation

Telephone language

Numbers and Symbols

Professional meetings

Important verbs

7

GIVING A PRESENTATION 1

If you are going to give a presentation of your company, a new product or system, you must provide the content of your talk. But using some of these professional phrases will provide a structure for your presentation and make it easier for your audience to follow what you say.

I'd like to
- begin by showing you...
- demonstrate....
- suggest some distinct advantages (of the new model)
- invite you to raise any questions now.
- close by saying.....

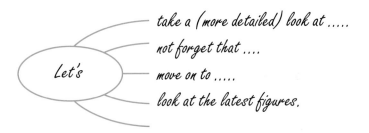

Let's
- take a (more detailed) look at .....
- not forget that ....
- move on to .....
- look at the latest figures.

Write some sentences you could use in a presentation of your own.

_____

_____

_____

_____

_____

_____

_____

_____

GIVING A PRESENTATION 2

These professional phrases will help you to structure a presentation in English. Make sure you know how each one is used. It might help to add translations.

As
- you can see . . .
- I will explain . . .
- I have explained . . .
- you know, . . .
- this diagram shows . . .

I should
- point out that . . .
- explain that . . .
- emphasise that . . .
- remind you that . . .
- add that . . .

7

Write some sentences you could use in a presentation. Remember that writing your own sentences will make it easier to remember the important language. If you need to make a presentation, it will help to write full notes, and to include these phrases, not just the language you need to talk about your own business. Recording the presentation and listening to yourself will help you to feel more confident when you give the presentation to a real audience.

TELEPHONE LANGUAGE 1

There are a few expressions which are standard on the telephone. Here are the most useful:

INTRODUCTION

This is ..... Could I speak to Mr(s) ..... please?

Speaking. (when you are the person someone asks for. It means 'That's me')

Just a moment, please. I'll put you through.

MESSAGES

Could I leave a message, please?

Could you ask him/her to call me back, please?

Would you like to leave a message?

Shall I ask him/her to call you back?   Has (s)he got your number?

REQUESTS ABOUT THE PHONE

Could I use your phone, please?

Could I call my office, please?

Could you get me the number/code for ....., please?

REQUESTS ON THE PHONE

Could I speak to ...?

Extension (four seven three) please.

Could you tell (....) that (your name) called, please?

NEGATIVE RESPONSES

I'm afraid (s)he's   not in the office at the moment.
out for lunch.
in a meeting.
on holiday.
rather tied up at the moment.
no longer with us. Can someone else help you?
on another line.

Remember how important **I'm afraid** is in giving negative responses. (See page 29)

TELEPHONE LANGUAGE 2

In many places in this book we explain how important word partnerships are. The most important word for talking about the telephone is **call**. It can be a noun or a verb. It makes lots of important partnerships. Here are the most useful.

a local call	**to call (someone) back**
a long-distance call	**to call the office**
to pay for the call	**to call my wife/the office**
Can I call direct?	**to call New York/Tokyo**
I'm in a call box.	**I'll call you next week.**

Here are some more important 'telephone' words and expressions.

The line is engaged.

The line is out of order.

It's a very bad line. Can I call you back?

Have you the code for (Milan) please?

The receiver is off the hook.

I'm sorry, I think you must have the wrong number.

I'm afraid there's no one of that name here.

FINISHING A CALL

Sometimes it is difficult to show you are ready to finish. Many British people pause, then say **"Anyway....."** followed by another short pause. It gives the other person a chance to add something if they want and to show they are ready to finish too. Often if you are asked about something you finish with **"Right, I'll get back to you soon/next week/as soon as I can"**.

NUMBERS

British people usually give telephone numbers one digit at a time, except for 'doubles':

327904	**three two, seven nine, oh four**
226433	**double two, six four, double three**

Note: American 'telephone talk' is sometimes different from British English. The most important difference is a fixed expression with two completely different meanings:

A British operator says *"Are you through?"* to check you are successfully connected. Your call has just **started.**

An American operator says *"Are you through?"* to check that you have finished what you wanted to say. Your call has just **finished.**

7

NUMBERS AND SYMBOLS 1

Most business people need to say certain numbers, symbols and abbreviations. Here is a list of important ones. Say them several times so they feel comfortable when you say them.

YOU WRITE	YOU SAY
3/8	three eighths
0.27	nought point two seven
304	three oh four (for hotel rooms, notice '0' is usually 'oh')
1992	nineteen ninety two (for the year)
6 June	the sixth of June
6.30pm	six thirty p.m. or half past six (in the evening)
13%	thirteen percent

WEIGHTS AND DIMENSIONS

3cm x 8cm	three (centimetres) by eight (centimetres)
3m²	three square metres
2kg.	two kilos
$^1/_2$lb.	half a pound (notice the 'a')
3cu.m.	three cubic metres
£2/kg.	two pounds per kilo

ABBREVIATIONS

These are said one letter at a time. Here are a few with their meanings.

plc	public limited company
fob	free on board
TVA	French VAT (Value added tax)
EC	European Community (sometimes called 'The Common Market')
USSR	The Soviet Union (often, wrongly, called 'Russia')

NUMBERS AND SYMBOLS 2

Each person has different needs for the signs, symbols and abbreviations that will be most important to them. Use these headings to list the ones which will be most use to you.

Spell your name, your company name, address etc.

Give important phone numbers naturally (see page 133)

Important products   Finance   Organisations

YOU WRITE   **YOU SAY**

7

PROFESSIONAL MEETINGS 1

If you are at a meeting with several people present, it will help you to present your ideas if you use the natural expressions which structure your contribution. Check the expressions on these two pages. Make sure you understand how they are used. Choose the ones you feel comfortable with. Say them several times. Record them, then listen to yourself.

BEGINNING

I'd like to make several points . . . firstly . . .

I'd like to begin by . . . ing.

ASKING FOR AN OPINION

What's your opinion of . . .

What's your position/view on . . .

GIVING AN OPINION

I believe/think/feel that . . .

In my opinion/view . . .

AGREEING

I agree entirely/completely.

I think we are in agreement on that.

AGREEING PARTIALLY

I would tend to agree with you on that.

I agree with you on the whole, but . . .

DISAGREEING TACTFULLY

I agree up to a point, but . . .

To a certain extent I agree with you, but . . .

I'm sorry but I really can't agree with you on that.

INTERRUPTING

If I may just interrupt you for a moment, I'd like to . . .

I don't want to interrupt, but can I just say that . . .

PROFESSIONAL MEETINGS 2

TAKING CONTROL OF THE DISCUSSION

Could I come in there for a moment, please?

Could I just make a few comments, please.

SAYING NOTHING

I'm afraid I can't comment on that yet/at this stage.

It's very difficult to say (at the moment).

MISUNDERSTANDINGS

I'm afraid there seems to be some misunderstanding . . . . Perhaps I can clarify what I said . . .

BLOCKING

I can see a lot of difficulties with that suggestion/proposal.

Could you explain in a little more detail, please.

I'm still rather unhappy about . . .

EXPRESSING YOUR VIEWS

That suggestion/proposal has my full support.

I suggest/propose that . . .

Don't you agree that . . . needs to be considered?

We would be happy to . . . if you were willing to . . .

I (particularly) want to emphasise/highlight the fact that . . .

CLOSING

To sum up, . . .

Finally, . . .

Let me conclude by stressing once again/saying . . .

Make sure you feel comfortable saying these expressions before you try to use them in an important business meeting.

IMPORTANT VERBS 1

Often the words which you think are most important for you are nouns, for example, **meeting, sales, insurance**. But if you want to speak English you need to speak and write sentences. So, you need to know which verbs are often used with your important nouns and with word partnerships which include the noun. Here are some examples:

attend a meeting	**organise a meeting**	**postpone a meeting**
increase sales	**achieve a sales target**	**launch a sales campaign**
take out insurance	**pay an insurance premium**	**make an insurance claim**

These two and three-word combinations are often the basis of complete sentences in business English.

A good business English dictionary will help you with the important nouns but very often it does not help you to choose the correct verb to make important word partnerships. On the following pages is a list of some of the verbs which are often used in professional English. You can use the list in two different ways:

1. Take a key word. Look for verbs which are often used with the keyword. List the most useful word partnerships.

2. Choose an area of professional English, for example **banking, insurance,** or **exports.** Look for verbs which will make word partnerships connected with that area. Make a list, with equivalents in your own language.

On the opposite page you will see an example. All professionals need to talk about **meetings.** But which **verbs** do you need to help you to do this. The most important ones are listed.

Use the following pages to make similar lists starting from the key words or professional areas which **you** need.

7

IMPORTANT VERBS 2

Most professionals need to talk about meetings. You almost certainly know the word. But which verbs make word partnerships with it? A business dictionary and the verb list on pages 144 to 146 will help you to find partnerships and equivalents in your own language. Check later by covering the English column to make sure you can remember.

ENGLISH	YOUR LANGUAGE / EXAMPLE
address a meeting	
arrange a meeting	
ask for a meeting	
attend a meeting	
avoid a meeting	
be late for a meeting	
be tied up in a meeting	
call a meeting	
cancel a meeting	
chair a meeting	
close a meeting	
have a meeting	
interrupt a meeting	
organise a meeting	
postpone a meeting	
report on a meeting	
set up a meeting	
start a meeting	
take the minutes of a meeting	
wind up a meeting	

7

IMPORTANT VERBS 3

Choose a **key word** and write it here: _____

Use the verb list on page 144 / 6 and a business dictionary to find useful word partnerships.

List them with equivalents in your language or English examples.

WORD PARTNERSHIPS	YOUR LANGUAGE / EXAMPLE
_____	_____
_____	_____
_____	_____
_____	_____
_____	_____
_____	_____
_____	_____
_____	_____
_____	_____
_____	_____
_____	_____
_____	_____
_____	_____
_____	_____
_____	_____
_____	_____

7

IMPORTANT VERBS 4

Choose a **key word** and write it here: _____

Use the verb list and a business dictionary to find useful word partnerships.

List them with equivalents in your language or English examples.

WORD PARTNERSHIPS	YOUR LANGUAGE / EXAMPLE

IMPORTANT VERBS 5

Write a **professional area** useful to you here: _____

Use the list and a business dictionary to find and list useful word partnerships with equivalents in your own language or English examples.

WORD PARTNERSHIPS   YOUR LANGUAGE / EXAMPLE

7

IMPORTANT VERBS 6

Write a **professional area** useful to you here: _____

Use the list and a business dictionary to find and list useful word partnerships with equivalents in your own language or English examples.

WORD PARTNERSHIPS   YOUR LANGUAGE / EXAMPLE

7

LIST OF IMPORTANT VERBS

The following verbs are all common in professional English. Verbs which are marked * are verbs which are often used as part of two-word verbs like **take on, set up.**

A bsorb	accept	account for	accumulate	achieve
acknowledge	acquire	add	address	adjust
adopt	advertise	afford	advise	agree
aim	allocate	allow	analyse	announce
apologise	apply	appoint	appreciate	approach
approve	argue	arrange	ask	assemble
assess	assist	attempt	attend	attract
audit	authorise	avoid		

B ackdate	balance	bank	bargain	base
beat	become	begin	believe	benefit
bid	blame	block	book	boost
borrow	break*	bring*	budget	build
buy				

C alculate	call*	campaign	cancel	capitalise on
capture	carry*	centralise	chair	change
charge	chase	cheat	check	choose
claim	clear	close	collaborate with	collect
combine	commit	communicate	compare	compensate
compete with	complain	compromise	con	concede
conclude	conduct	confirm	confuse	congratulate
connect	conserve	consider	consign	consult
consume	contact	continue	contract	control
convert	copy	correct	cost	cover
credit				

D amage	date	debit	decide	declare
decline	deduct	defeat	defend	deflate
delay	delegate	delete	deliver	demand
demonstrate	demote	de-nationalise	depart from	deposit
depreciate	depress	de-regulate	design	describe
detail	devalue	develop	direct	discover
discuss	dismiss	dispatch	display	dissolve
distinguish	diversify	divide	downgrade	draft
draw up	drop	duplicate		

E arn	economise	elect	employ	enclose
encourage	endorse	enforce	enquire	enter
entertain	equip	escape	establish	estimate
evade	evaluate	exceed	exchange	exclude
execute	exercise	exhibit	expand	expect
expire	explain	export	express	extend
extract				

7

LIST OF IMPORTANT VERBS

F ace / fail / fake / fall / falsify
favour / fax / feel / fetch / fiddle
figure out / fill in / finalise / finance / find
fine / finish / fix / float / fly
fold / follow / force / forecast / forget
form / forward / freeze / fulfil / fund
furnish

G ain / gather / gear / generate / get*
give* / go* / govern / grant / greet
group / grow / guarantee / guess

H aggle / halt / hand in / handle / harm
hedge / help / hire / hit / hold*
hurry / hurt

I mplement / imply / import / impose / improve
increase / incur / indicate / inform / inflate
influence / inherit / insert / insist on / inspect
instal / instruct / insure / integrate / intend
interfere with / interpret / introduce / invent / invest in
investigate / invite / invoice / issue

J oin / joke / judge

K eep / know

L abel / launch / lay off / lead / learn
lease / leave / legalise / lend / license
lift / limit / link / listen to / loan
lock / lose / lower

M ail / maintain / make* / man / manage
manufacture / market / maximise / mean / measure
meet / merge / minimise / miscalculate / mismanage
misunderstand / modify / move / mortgage / motivate
multiply

N ationalise / neglect / negotiate / net / nominate
note / notice / notify / number

O bject to / obtain / offer / offload / omit
open / operate / oppose / order / organise
outbid / outdo / outsell / outvote / own
overcharge / overestimate / overheat / overvalue / overwork

P ack / package / patent / pay* / peak
peg / penalise / penetrate / perform / permit
persuade / phone / pick* / pin down / place

7

LIST OF IMPORTANT VERBS

plan	plough back	point out	pollute	post
predict	prefer	prepare	present	press
pretend	prevent	price	print	privatise
produce	prohibit	promote	prompt	propose
protect	provide	publicise	publish	purchase
Qualify	question	queue	quote	
Raise	rally	reach	react	read
realise	reassure	recall	receive	recognise
recommend	reconcile	record	recover	recruit
re-cycle	redeem	re-distribute	re-draft	reduce
refer to	refund	refuse	register	regret
regulate	release	rely on	remain	remember
remind	remove	renew	rent	re-organise
re-pay	repeat	replace	reply	report
re-possess	represent	request	require	rescue
research	reserve	resign	resist	resolve
respect	restrict	re-structure	retain	retire
return	re-value	review	revise	roll over
run*	rush			
Satisfy	save	say	schedule	secure
sell*	send	separate	settle	shake up
share	shelve	ship	show	shut down
sign	simplify	sink	slash	slow
smuggle	soar	solve	sort out	specialise in
specify	speculate	spend	split	spread
stabilise	staff	stamp	standardise	start up
state	stay	steal	stick to	stock
store	streamline	strike	structure	study
subcontract	submit	subscribe to	subsidise	succeed
sue	suffer	suggest	suit	supervise
supply	support	survey		
Talk	take*	target	tax	telephone
telex	tell	terminate	test	top up
trade	train	transfer	translate	transport
travel	trust	turn*	type	
Under-charge	undercut	undermine	undervalue	underwrite
understand	up-date	upgrade	use	utilise
Value	vary	verify	view	vote
Want	warn	warrant	waste	weigh up
welcome	win	wind up	withdraw from	withhold
work*	work out	wreck	write	
Yield				

INTRODUCTION

Successful international business means communicating with people from different cultural backgrounds. People not only have different language backgrounds, but also very different cultural backgrounds. We all look at the world from the perspective of our own culture. Often we are surprised that other cultures have very different perspectives. These differences can be exciting and stimulating — part of the reason for visiting foreign countries on holiday. They can also be puzzling and frustrating — 'Why do **these people** always say one thing and do something completely different?'. Sometimes in international business a breakdown in communication happens and neither side really knows what has gone wrong or why it has gone wrong.

Obviously, if you are planning to do a lot of business with one particular foreign culture, it is useful to learn as much as possible about ways of doing business in that culture. Some points may be 'easy to learn' — in the Christian world offices are usually closed on Sundays, but in the Moslem world on Fridays. Other points may be more 'difficult to learn' — in Britain it is not usual for two businessmen to embrace each other on meeting but in some Latin American cultures it is.

If you are planning to do business cross-culturally the most helpful first step is to learn more about **your own** cultural assumptions. The way we accept as the **normal** way of approaching a situation may in fact be very bound to our own cultural background. The purpose of these pages is to help you focus on basic assumptions about everyday business situations. We hope that the exercises will raise many questions in your mind. It is best to approach a foreign culture with an open and questioning mind.

8

TIME

Doing business involves organising time. Ways of organising time differ a lot from culture to culture. At what time should you meet? How long should a meeting last? etc. Check your assumptions here. Mark the **Yes** or **No** box for each question.

	YES	NO
It would be unusual for me to have a first business appointment before 9.30am.	☐	☐
I often organise a business lunch for 11.30.	☐	☐
My business lunches normally last about $1\frac{1}{2}$ hours.	☐	☐
I normally expect to stay in the office until about 6.30pm.	☐	☐
I never make business phone calls before 9am.	☐	☐
I stay in the office to work after the office closes quite often.	☐	☐
If a business partner arrives 10 minutes late for an appointment this is no real problem.	☐	☐
If I am invited for drinks to a business partner's home for 8pm I would usually arrive at 8.05.	☐	☐

Do you feel that your choices are very different from the choices a person from another country would make? Have you ever had any particular problems arising from different attitudes to time?

8

DRESS

Choice of dress is of course a personal matter. But it is also influenced by national culture, company culture and occupational culture. Check your own ideas here. Mark the **Agree** or **Disagree** box for each statement.

	AGREE	DISAGREE
I always wear a dark suit when attending a business meeting.	☐	☐
During a meeting I often take my jacket off.		
a) to be more comfortable.	☐	☐
b) to create a more relaxed atmosphere.	☐	☐
Wearing good quality, expensive clothes for important meetings is essential.	☐	☐
Sometimes it may be quite appropriate to wear smart casual clothes for a meeting.	☐	☐
I usually try to wear one item of clothing which carries the name or logo of my company.	☐	☐
If a business partner suggested going for a swim or a sauna together I would		
a) be surprised.	☐	☐
b) feel uncomfortable and refuse.	☐	☐
If I am invited to a business partner's home for a meal I would wear the same type of clothes as to the office.	☐	☐

8

When doing business internationally have you noticed any major differences between your dress assumptions and those of your partners? If there have been differences have you ever felt uncomfortable because of these?

BUSINESS MEETINGS

Not everybody does business in the same way. Some differences are personal but some are cultural. It helps if you have thought about what you expect and if you understand that people from other countries may have different expectations.

Which of the following topics might you talk about during a **first business meeting** with people from a new company that you hope to do business with regularly in the future?

In a $3\frac{1}{2}$ hour meeting how much time could be given to each topic that you choose? Complete the table with **your** expectations.

        Pricing   **Products or services**

The architecture   **The weather**   **Sport**
of the host's city

      Family and private interests   **Previous business experience**
                                         in the country

TOPIC	TIME

Are there any other topics you would definitely expect to discuss in a first business meeting? If so, include them in the table with an estimate of the time you would give to each topic.

NEGOTIATION

Most professional people have to take part in negotiations from time to time. Of course, different people negotiate in different ways. It is partly a matter of personality. But we also make assumptions which are part of our background – about the way things are 'usually' done. But this often only means 'usually done where I come from'. Check your assumptions here. Mark the **Yes** or **No** box for each question.

In a negotiation do you:

	YES	NO
Get to know and use the first names of the people from the other side to establish a good climate?	☐	☐
Have periods of silence to think about the issues?	☐	☐
Use 'bargaining' techniques to arrive at a mutually acceptable price?	☐	☐
Ever say (the single word) 'No'?	☐	☐
Include unnecessary conditions so you can seem helpful and reasonable when you drop them.	☐	☐
Continue important, substantive discussions in a social setting, for example a restaurant?	☐	☐
Try always to get a written, signed agreement – in other words, a contract?	☐	☐
Include technical and legal specialists in your negotiating team?	☐	☐

Do you think the choices you have made are the same choices that people from another company or another country that you do business with would make? Have you ever felt uncomfortable because of the way others negotiated with you? Can you say why?

ORGANISATIONS

Every professional needs to be organised, but not everyone sees organisation in the same way. Different cultures have different values. These values affect the way we think and work in organisations. Check your own ideas. Mark the **Agree** or **Disagree** box for each statement.

	AGREE	**DISAGREE**
In an organisation, managers should be able to answer all their subordinates' questions.	☐	☐
In an organisation, group work is generally more productive than individual work.	☐	☐
Achieving power in an organisation is as important as achieving business objectives.	☐	☐
Conflict is a negative factor in organisations.	☐	☐
It is important for everyone in a company to know exactly who is reponsible for what. Everyone needs to know the company structure clearly.	☐	☐
As far as possible a company should treat all its employees, from the least to the most important in a similar way.	☐	☐
The most effective organisations include **both** women and men side-by-side in their management structure.	☐	☐
Companies should have a way of finding out what subordinates really think of their boss(es).	☐	☐

How many of the answers you have given are typical for **most** business people in your country? Do you think your international business colleagues would give the same answers?

8

PRESENTATIONS

There are of course many factors which influence the style of a **Presentation:** what is the purpose of the presentation, how many people are in the audience, how 'formal' is the overall situation? etc. Another significant factor is the country and culture where the presentation is being made.

Check your own assumptions here. When you give a presentation in **your** culture, which of the following do you do? Choose and put in sequence. If any steps are missing add them in yourself.

Tell a joke.

Make a general statement about the subject.

Refer to visuals.

Ask the audience to introduce themselves.

Ask questions.

Summarise.

State your objectives.

Smile at the audience.

Take your jacket off.

Look serious to inspire confidence.

8

From your own experience of attending presentations have you noticed any major differences in national styles?

FORMAL MEETINGS 1

The language used in formal meetings is very standard. The same expressions are almost always used.

On these two pages we usually give two expressions in each section. The first is the standard formal use; the second is more informal but still used in meetings conducted in the formal style. The sections marked * are for use by the Chairman.

In all cases, instead of *Chairman* some people now prefer to use *Chairwoman*, or *the Chair*. In a formal meeting we suggest you agree which use the people at the meeting, particularly the person in the chair, prefer.

OPENING *

Ladies and Gentleman, I declare the meeting open.
Right, shall we get started.

MINUTES *

Would someone move that the minutes of the last meeting be accepted?
Can we take the minutes as read?

AGENDA *

Has everyone received a copy of the agenda? The first item is . . .

INVITING A SPEAKER *

(Mr Barnard), would you like to say something about this?
Have you anything to say, (John).

ASKING TO COMMENT

Excuse me, Mr Chairman, may I say something, please?
Could I just say something here, please.

FINISHING AN AGENDA ITEM *

Has anyone anything else they wish to add before we move on to the next item on the agenda?
Has anyone anything further to add?

CONTROLLING THE SUBJECT *

I don't think that is relevant at the moment. The main question is . . .
Let's not get side-tracked. Could you stick to the subject, please?

NAMING A SINGLE SPEAKER *

We can't all speak at the same time. Would you like to comment first, Mrs Hill?

8

FORMAL MEETINGS 2

MOVING ON *
Could we move on to item (3) on the agenda?
Can we go on now to...

POSTPONING DISCUSSION *
If nobody objects, I suggest we leave this matter until (our next meeting/a later date.)
Perhaps we could leave this for the time being. We can come back to it later.

PROPOSING
I'd like to propose that ...

SECONDING
(Chair) Would anyone like to second that?
(Others) Mr Chairman, I'll second that motion.

ANNOUNCING A VOTE *
Perhaps we should take a formal vote on this. Can I ask for a show of hands?
Could we take a vote on that?

VOTING * (All formal for the Chair)
Those in favour of the motion, please?
Those against?
Any abstentions?
The motion is carried unanimously/by six votes to three.

The motion has been rejected overwhelmingly/by six votes to three.

AGREEING WITHOUT A FORMAL VOTE *
Can I take it everyone is in favour of that, then?
Are we all agreed on that?

ANY OTHER BUSINESS *
Is there any other business?
Any further points (anyone wants to bring up)?

CLOSING THE MEETING *
I declare the meeting closed. Thank you everybody.
That's all for today. Thank you.

Y ou may find it helpful to think about some of the questions on pages 150 and 151 if you
have to attend formal meetings conducted in English.

8

CASE STUDY 1

Mike Brown is a recently appointed project manager with Western Paints — a US company with subsidiaries around the world. The job is giving him his first experience of managing a culturally diverse group. His project team consists of two Americans, a Japanese, a Swede and an Italian. Mike himself is American.

At a recent meeting of the group Mike gave an outline of some proposed deadlines and tasks. "A lot of work has to be done during these next two weeks," he explained. "It means we will have to work over the weekend in order to finish this important report. Let's now divide up the work and then go away and do it."

Mike was surprised when Sven Lindberg, the Swedish member of the group, seemed unhappy about working over the weekend. Another problem was that both Takahiro Miki (Japanese) and Marco Venditti (Italian) were unsure about how to do their parts of the report.

Mike believes that he is a good manager of people. He has been responsible for many different groups of people in the United States and has never had any real problems in motivating people to work.

On the Friday evening after the meeting he went home and talked about the situation with his wife. "I just don't know the best way to motivate these foreigners," he said. "Maybe they want me to organise a party for them — make them feel good. We'll have a meal here in our house one evening and invite them all."

So Mike and his wife Carol organised a dinner party for the group members and their wives. Everyone came but nobody seemed to enjoy themselves very much. It was very difficult to find topics of conversation to interest people — unusual for Mike. Marco's wife spoke only a little English which was another problem. All the guests left quite early and Mike was not very optimistic about the next day at work.

Have you been in any situation like this?

What do you think is the problem?

Do you think the reactions of Mike, Sven, Takahiro and Marco will be the same? If not, why not?

CASE STUDY 2

Can you match the comments with the people? Can you give reasons for your choices?

Sven Lindberg

Marco Venditti

Mike Brown

Takahiro Miki

	WHO?	WHY?
"Mike Brown should make more decisions. He's the manager. He's not paid to ask us questions. We need to know what to do."		
"I can't work with people who have a 'nine-to-five' approach."		
"These Americans are only interested in doing the job. What about my family? It's not fair to them if I have to work in my free time."		
"I don't like the responsibility of writing this report myself. Why can't we do it as a group? After all we are a project team."		
"Why should I call him 'Mike'? I'm not interested in parties in his house. He's my boss not my friend!"		

Have you worked with any Swedes, Japanese, Italians or Americans yourself? Were they "typical"?

8

STEREOTYPES

As Mike Brown has discovered there are often problems in managing a multinational team of people. For example the American emphasis on the individual is very different from the Japanese wish to work as a member of a group. The Swedish desire to balance business and private life may give Americans the idea that they are not committed to work. For some cultures home and culture are clearly separate. Inviting colleagues to your home may not be seen as a welcoming gesture.

Choose **one** of the following cultural groups. Do not choose your own culture. Write 5 or 6 words that you think describe the members of this culture.

Americans   **Italians**   **British**   **Swedes**   **Japanese**

National Group	

Now choose a national group that your company often does business with. Write some words to describe that nationality.

National Group	

How many of your descriptions are positive words? How many are negative? Very often our **stereotypes** are negative and not positive. This can be dangerous if it influences our decisions.

Now write the names of 3 of your **foreign business partners** here. Also their nationalities. Are they "typical"?

_____   _____   _____

Stereotypes can be dangerous. If you work with multinational groups it is important to learn as much as possible about the cultural expectations of the members. In this way differences can become **advantages** and not disadvantages.

DIFFICULT SITUATIONS

Difficult situations are even more difficult when doing business with people from other cultures. They may not recognise your 'signals'. You may not recognise their signals.

Check some of your ideas here. Mark the **Yes** or **No** box for each statement.

	YES	NO
When people mean "No" I expect them to say "No", politely but directly.	☐	☐
I like to stay relatively silent when a business partner is explaining a proposal. This shows that I am interested and respect their ideas.	☐	☐
If they won't call me by my first name then they probably don't like my ideas and don't really want to build a business relationship.	☐	☐
The words people use are so important that it is necessary to agree everything in writing.	☐	☐
The best way to show a deal has been agreed is to have a drink together.	☐	☐
If I am one of four people at a business dinner, I expect to pay a quarter of the bill.	☐	☐

If you disagreed with any of these statements, what was **your** expectation? Do you think other nationalities would have very different expectations?

8

This book cannot give answers for how every different culture thinks about different situations. The **Cultural Background** pages are to help you to understand that what **you** expect may be quite different from what **other people** expect. It is easier to avoid misunderstandings if you realise in advance that they might happen.